Action
Theater

Action Theater

THE IMPROVISATION
OF PRESENCE

Ruth
Zaporah

North Atlantic Books
Berkeley, California

Published by
North Atlantic Books
P.O. Box 12327
Berkeley, CA 94712

Cover photograph by Frank Werblin
Cover and book design by Paula Morrison
Typeset by Catherine Campaigne
Printed in the United States of America by Malloy Lithographing

Action Theater: The Improvisation of Presence is sponsored by the Society for the Study of Native Arts and Sciences, a nonprofit educational corporation whose goals are to develop an educational and crosscultural perspective linking various scientific, social, and artistic fields; to nurture a holistic view of the arts, sciences, humanities, and healing; and to publish and distribute literature on the relationship of mind, body, and nature.

Library of Congress Cataloguing-in-Publication Data
Zaporah, Ruth, 1936–
    Action theater : the improvisation of presence / Ruth Zaporah.
        p. cm.
      ISBN 1-55643-186-4
      1. Improvisation (Acting) 2. Theater I. Title.
    PN2071.I5Z36 1995
    792'.028—dc20   94-19401
                                                            CIP

1 2 3 4 5 6 7 8 9 / 98 97 96 95

This book is for my parents,
Ethel and Henry.
They never forgot
To ask me to dance.

Acknowledgements

I want to express my deep gratitude to Sten Rudstrom who, by my side at the computer, diligently corrected and polished every word, sentence and paragraph. Sten taught me to hear and create a beautiful sentence. He challenged me to clarity and guided me to completion.

I thank Maria St. John for those innumerable interviews with the tape recorder and her organizational and conceptual genius. I thank Ruth Mathews for her flow charts, her challenges and her faith in me as her teacher.

I'm grateful all the folks who patiently trained with me knowing that where we were going was a mystery to all of us.

I thank Barbara Green, Dadie Donnelly, and Frank Werblin for reading pieces of the manuscript and encouraging me to go on. I thank Will Smolak for his friendship and his fierce search for freedom, Joan Kennedy White, who co-created some of the early improvisational teaching and performance investigations during the raw and bumbling years, Molly Sullivan, who showed up for those early classes when no one else did, Stephen Heffernan, for the talks out in the clover field, Al Wunder for being my one and only improvisation mentor, Terry Sendgraff, for sharing two studios, many struggles and much love, Cynthia Moore, who was willing to risk performing improvisationally with me, Bob Ernst, for being my improvisation partner for many years and sharing his musical chops and actorly talents with me, Tony Montanero, who first said "Make it up." Nancy Stark Smith and Lisa Nelson who generously provide a forum, Contact Quarterly, for improvisation publications, and again Nancy for prodding my philosophical psyche, Rinde Eckert, Susan Griffin, Mary Forcade, Ellen Webb, and Rhiannon for sharing their masterful talents with me in performance and for showing confidence and appreciation in my work, and to Robert Hurwitt for his critical understanding and support when some of us were trying to figure out what improvisation performance was all about.

I thank my sons and daughter, Eric, Emily, Zac, and Jake, for allowing me to parent them untraditionally and at odd hours. Without their adaptable natures and good heartedness, particularly during those late night mailings and production emergencies, Action Theater would not have happened.

The most recent photos in this book are the work of my friend and most gifted photographer, Jan Watson. I am truly grateful for her patient and discerning eye. Other photographers whose work appears on these pages are Greg Peterson, Dianne Coleman, Sabine von der Tann, Annie Bates-Winship, and Roberto Cavanna.

I am indebted to the students and colleagues who appear throughout this book, either in photographic image or anecdote. I hope this book warms their hearts as they have warmed mine.

Finally, I thank Lindy Hough, my editor at North Atlantic Books, for her encouragement, support, understanding and love of dance and theater.

Contents

Foreword

by Barbara Dilley

The first time I saw Ruth Zaporah perform my mind stopped. I had to give up figuring it out. Each moment unfolded from the moment before, flavored with outrageousness and with haunting familiarity. I watched her face, eyes, mouth, hands; heard her voice move from language I knew to speaking in tongues. And I "knew" what she was revealing: I "knew" how it was, with her, and with me She was showing me something I already "knew" yet saw as if for the first time. Ruth is a master improvisator.

The art of improvisation is rooted in many world traditions; the ragas of India begin with the musicians tuning their instruments to the vibrations of the room and of the audience; the venerable clown traditions are full of improvising with audiences and telling stories that make fun of the locals; the shadow plays of Indonesia and Bali create current political satire and up-to-date town gossip from the Ramayana epic; the troupe of actors in Hamlet improvise their drama so as to expose a murder.

Here, in the States, our mighty tradition of jazz, unique to our African American history, has inspired a new understanding of musical soul. Songs become structures and playgrounds for hearts to soar to the stars then drop back into the chorus for one last round. These expressions of human vastness and every day magic arose for one reason—the love of it; that wild taste of delight that comes from making it up, on the spot, feeling the connection to hearts and minds across time.

Improvisation has long been part of the training of artists of all persuasions:

"Let go."
"Play with it."
"Don't think."
"Use what you have."

"Make it up as you go along."

This is the language in classrooms, studios, and stages where teachers pass on the secrets of creativity. At The Naropa Institute, where I teach and where I first saw Ruth perform, teachers such as Allen Ginsberg, Anne Waldman in poetry, Meredith Monk, Naomi Newman in theater and Art Lande and Jerry Granelli in music call forth the muses of creative imagination through the practices of improvisation. They offer unique structures and different languages but it all points to the same moment—when communication electrifies the air.

In the past thirty years, there has been an increase of improvisation by performing artists. Not only the jazz musicians but actors, dancers and performance artists have chosen to create games and structures that hold their intent together with the spontaneity of the moment. Since the 1960s when all the frontiers of consciousness were explored for their creative power, the act of performing improvisation became a guaranteed ride full of this wild taste of spontaneous delight. Everything was asked of you, moment by moment, over and over, again. Both artists and audiences felt the atmosphere when this surge of creative revelation flowed between them. Those of us who were trained in traditional forms of dance and theater were released into delicious rule-breaking. We suddenly found the mother lode of our creative power by putting ourselves in situations of risk, and uncertainty, and fearlessly staying awake. Improvisation is, as Gertrude Stein says so well, "Using everything, beginning again and again, and a continuous present."

Most of everything I have today in the way of improvisational "chops" comes from the years between 1969–1976 spent evolving out of Yvonne Rainer's "Continuous Project Altered Daily" into The Grand Union, that great circus of improvisational performance. Steve Paxton, Trisha Brown, David Gordon, Nancy Lewis, Douglas Dunn, myself, and others from time to time began the extraordinary saga of making it up as we went along, over and over again. After a few months of getting together diligently prior to a performance, we gave up rehearsing altogether. We just "began" when the curtain went up and the lights went on. I remember being shocked during performances by actions that my comrades made, only to recognize that the impulse they had followed had also been mine and I had repressed it. The next time, I opened to that impulse and ran with it. And my friends followed my lead. Such kinesthetic joy!

Only after this first flush had passed were we to struggle to understand how to proceed. "Trying" to be spontaneous is a horrid and grossly self-conscious experience. Everyone who values the insight and challenge of improvisation meets this monster. It is Ruth's gift to us in this book to create a training that gently, but firmly, points out this dilemma and then teaches us how to move through, even use it. I can hear her now, "That's it. That's it. Just use it. Whatever it is. Use the energy. Ride it."

Nothing offered those of us fascinated by the art and practice of improvisation a language and an understanding of this process of perceptual spontaneity like the teachings of meditation and awareness practice from the Buddhist tradition. It's an intriguing story. From the beginning of the twentieth century, teachers of the great wisdom traditions of the east have brought their insight into the nature of mind and the phenomena of the senses to this country. Buddhism is a magnificent philosophy and has a tradition of deeply studying the mind and sense perceptions. Buddhist philosophy posits a sixth sense perception—the perception of mind and the process of thinking—to add to the basic five perceptions of seeing, hearing, smelling, tasting and touching. It gives us a language to investigate the experience of impulse. Buddhist meditation is a mind training. It trains us to discriminate, to pick up and put down the myriad impulses that enter our bodies every day. We slow our thinking and perceiving down and watch/feel our world arise, dwell and disappear. The experience of our world becomes vivid and energetic. As a discipline, meditation always asks us to come back to the breath, to return to the body and to listen to the body, to what it is "saying," what is being experienced, right now. By disciplining our awareness of these six perceptions, we hone and sharpen the tools we play with when we improvise.

Awareness is simple. Just notice, without bias, what is happening. "Pay attention." Rest the mind and let the senses be noticed. It seems easy. Everyone gets the idea. But it is hard to do. Over the decades, teachers, fellow practitioners and their books have investigated the practice of awareness. Agnes Martin, the brilliant, eccentric painter who fled New York in the late 50s wrote an essay about taming the dragon called Pride so that we can get to the creative expression we long to make. We can get the idea of awareness practice, but, day by day, hour by hour it can be impossible to "rest the mind."

With brilliant simplicity, Ruth brings her study and practice of awareness to the unique disciplines of Action Theater. She creates exercises with exacting clear intention that we can try out in the living room or kitchen. Here, the insistence on "bare attention" of the subtle shifts in body/mind dynamics and all its energies, its inner and outer landscapes, transforms our all-too-human foibles into breath-stopping insights and raucous humor. We take delight in making fun of ourselves. By following these exercises, we learn to be less afraid. We work side by side with others, exploring both the darker landscapes and the ridiculous risks of a fool. Ruth captures the nuances of perceptual experiences and invites us to play—for ourselves, for our creative delight no matter what use we make of it, and for others, whether we walk out the door with a splash of insightful humor or climb up on the stage to sing the blues.

For those of us who enter the teaching arena clutching our carpet bags of tricks and mirrors and minor illuminations to cull the creative spirit, Ruth describes a journey of discovery in "no-nonsense" language, and with deep intuition about human nature. These tools for the teaching art are woven into a tapestry of joyful disciplines, not only for performing artists but for each of us, living out our days full of missed opportunities for the wild delights of the unexpected, the delicious play of "making it up on the spot"—of improvising.

Barbara Dilley
Dance Movement Studies
The Naropa Institute
1995

Introduction

Dad initiated me into *seeing*. Sunday was his day to take the kids off my mother's hands. He and I would go to the park, or the bus station, or anyplace where there was a flow of people. We'd sit and watch folks pass by, and make up stories about them, attempting to guess their circumstances: Were they happy, Why or why not, what was their work, were they playful? Did they have a sense of humor? (Dad seemed to think this was very important.) Did they live alone? Did they have money? Were they honest, crooks, liars? We would imagine what it was like to be living in those bodies, shapes, weights, postures.

When I was 17, he gave me a book, *Autobiography of a Yogi* by Yogananda. Since then, books of that genre have been on my night table and their content has consumed my thoughts. The titles and authors have changed, as have the continents of origin—Western Europe, India, Japan, Tibet. But the substance remains the same. Who am I? What is experience? How do I proceed through this life? These inquiries, always stirring in the back of my mind, have influenced the way I've gone about making theater and devising this training. Not consciously, just as a whisper, choosing this over that.

I began dancing school at six—ballet, and then modern. I loved hard work, motion and silence. I loved dancing, saying I was dancing and being identified as "a dancer." I carried this personna into my early twenties, when I began to teach and choreograph, finally inventing for myself, finally feeling my own way.

In the mid 60s, a friend who was Chairman of a University Drama Department asked me to teach movement to the theater students. I accepted the job, naively thinking I would be teaching dance.

The first day, after greeting people, noticing how they were dressed, and how they behaved, I asked them what they wanted to learn. "To embody our characters," they said. Without a clear understanding of what that meant, I said, "Okay. Walk." After watching a few steps, I knew what my job was. These students had to get into their own bodies. They had to embody themselves before they could embody anybody else.

I began with simple explorations of ordinary tasks—walking, sitting, standing, reaching for things. We were improvising, even though "improvisation" hadn't come onto the scene yet, nor into my mind. I was making things up because that seemed to be the way to get things done. It wasn't long before I fell in love with the improvisation process, spontaneous expression, and the strange and graceful phenomena when the mind surprises itself.

In 1969, I moved to Berkeley, California, and joined the march toward feeling. My interest in improvisation really took off. It fit the climate of the territory and the times. Berkeley, too, was improvising: politically, socially, and psychologically. My students and I moved with the collective surge into the performing of the unknown.

For years I had been silent, but now, I opened my mouth. Voice was terrifying and seductive at the same time. I was off on a new course. Voice led to language, language to content and feeling. I was speaking and sounding, not just moving. Throughout these years, I was so dedicated to the discovery process that I isolated myself from my dance and theater colleagues, not peeking outside of my laboratory, not wanting to see what others were doing. It occurred to me that maybe I was reinventing the wheel. But I was on fire and it didn't matter.

I've spent the past thirty years investigating what I call Action Theater: the state of, and tactics for, body-based improvisational theater. I've done this by practicing, performing improvisationally and teaching students in my own classes, at theater, dance or art institutes in the United States and Europe, in psychological and spiritual centers. No matter who I work with, the situation is always the same. We all share a common and simple impediment: our judging minds. Regardless of our intentions in any situation, we haul around the past and future. To relax our attention into the present moment is extraordinarily simple, but, for most of us, it demands a lifetime of practice.

Action Theater: The Improvisation of Presence presents a month-long training, twenty work days of Action Theater. Each chapter reflects a single five-hour session of the training. The exercises for the day appear at the beginning of each chapter and are ordered developmentally. I provide instructions for every exercise and discuss their applications and implications. Occasionally, I add a story, anecdote, or metaphor. Like the practice, the writing of this book was in itself an improvisation. I began with the exercises and let them direct my thoughts. The chapters spun themselves out.

This book comprises an Action Theater awareness and performance training. It's a model, not just for performance but for life. It offers a way to proceed. Who we are, how we perceive our world, and how we respond to those perceptions are the same regardless of the surroundings. In the studio, we improvise within forms that are relevant to theater, but the lessons we learn effect our daily lives. The training is comprised of exercises and ideas that expand awareness, stimulate imagination, strengthen the capacity for feeling, and develop skills of expression. The rules defining the exercises are constraints that isolate components of human behavior. These rules open pathways that lead into unexplored territories where the mind and body rejoin, where there's no disparity between action and being.

The Action Theater exercises don't set up life-like "scenes." Instead, life-like and non-life-like situations arise through physical explorations within forms and frameworks. The forms are open, content-less, and address how we organize specific aspects of behavior or experience. They invite us to inhabit our bodies, deconstruct our normal behavior and, then, notice the details of what we've got. This process frees us from habitual perceptions and behaviors. We become more conscious of our moment to moment thoughts, sensations, emotions, feelings, and fantasies, in addition to the outer world we inhabit.

This practice turns the mind inside out. Because we place the activity of the mind into action, we can observe its ways, examine who we are and how we operate. We can consciously redirect our functioning.

This text offers an example of *one* twenty-day training of what I consider the basic work. When I teach my class the format follows no single tradition, neither dance nor theater. All of the participants are simultaneously active throughout each session. I rarely demonstrate anything. I watch, occasionally interrupting them to mention something I've noticed, or suggest they try a different approach. Usually, at the end of the session, small groups perform for the rest of the students.

I begin every session sitting in a circle with the participants. I sense the mood, the energy present and respond with the first exercise. Each class builds from what I see is happening or not happening, combined with the basic work that I intend to cover. The order is haphazard and immediate. I make up new exercises, veer off on tangents if need be. I watch the students and observe details. They teach me what to teach. Since every exercise has within it many teachings, what comes up each day and why it comes up, is dependent on what was occurring at that time. Every class is ideal, whether it's progressively arranged or scattered. Understanding the work comes with doing the exercises, regardless of what order they're done in. I purposefully say the same things over and over. I've done so in the book as well. As one progresses through the training, concepts understood early on ripen into deeper knowing. We learn through repetition. No matter how different the exercises look from each other, they're all about the same thing: presence.

The length of time students improvise on an exercise or score is variable. Usually, newer students have a shorter capacity to stay with an investigation. Their interest wanes due to the lack of skills. More experienced improvisers may stay with one exploration for hours. In class, I judge whether inaction or dullness is due to fear, boredom, laziness, distraction or lack of skill.

Some students arrive expecting to learn techniques that will turn them into charismatic performers, lawyers, teachers or parents. Soon, they learn that techniques bear limited fruit. At some point, we must look inward for our education. We must notice what inhibits our freedom, be willing to give up all preconceptions, be truthful, and relax in order to act from lively emptiness.

You need not be in a class, or even a member of a group, to benefit from the material in this book. Many of the exercises can be done alone or with a friend. No matter how they're practiced, they lead to the free expression of our constantly changing inner realities. They help us develop the ability to speak and be seen in all our aspects, to play and to connect with others.

Contradiction is inherent in the documenting or prescribing of improvised work. This book should be considered as a path of stones which lead in many directions, or a set of arrows that point to varied possible paths. You will undoubtedly take the precise path which you need to follow. That path will bring you home.

Form/Content

1A. On/Off Clothes
1B. Walk/Run/Freeze in Same Scene
1C. Move Same Time/Freeze Same Time
1D. Move at Different Times
1E. Performance Score: Autobiographies

The space is a large and sunny dance studio with a sprung wood floor. Mirrors run along one wall covered with white sheeting. Twenty students of varying ages and nationalities arrive. They change into their movement clothes and come out onto the floor. We sit in a circle, exchanging names, where each of us lives and a little information about what brought us to this training. I talk about our schedule, outlining our class times and discussion times. I tell them that they'll have fifteen minutes between the time they arrive and the time we form our opening circle to be on the floor, to stretch, sound, move or whatever it takes to relax.

I tell them that I will be telling them what to do for the next five hours. I tell them that most of the time they will be improvising on the floor rather than talking about improvising. I say that we will devote ourselves to the exploration of the phenomenon we call awareness. They will practice techniques to increase their skills of perception. We'll aware together.

1A. On/Off Clothes

• Everyone, put your street clothes back on. Change the speed of your movements as you handle your clothing. Sometimes move very quickly, sometimes slowly, sometimes pause altogether, stop moving, staccato movements, tremble, wave. Focus on each moment as it comes into your awareness. Even within a five second time frame, change your speed three or four times. Pretend that someone else is directing your movements, so that you are not thinking about it. Don't get serious. We're playing!!!

• Be aware of your eye focus. Choose what to look at. Do you always want to be looking down at the floor? You may want to look ahead of you, or behind you, or off to the side.

• Now, repeat this with half of the group watching, the other half doing.

＞ •

Dressing and undressing are conventions. They're movement patterns designed early in our lives, then repeated forever after. (Slip the shirt over the head first, then put the arms through. Put the right shoe on first. Button the jacket from the top down. Wet the toothbrush first, then apply the paste.)

These students had just come in off the street. The first thing they did was change their clothes. They were all experiencing some degree of excitement, since this was a new and unknown territory. They probably weren't paying too much attention to what they were doing and how they were doing it.

In **On/Off Clothes**, students look at a common experience in an uncommon way. They *play* with what they've always assumed was not play by focusing on the sensations of each moment of experience. How are they doing what they're doing, exactly? Are they moving in a heavy way, slowly or frantically fast? Do the clothes thud to the floor or gracefully cascade down? Students feel their way, feel the textures of their clothing, as they pull, slap, or slide them on or off. They unglue from the "getting dressed" idea, relate to the **form** of the action and the details inside of it. The forgotten comes to the surface; the conventional method of getting dressed/undressed is a living experience.

An activity can be experienced as a partnership between **form** and **content.** The **form** is the physical structuring, how the action shapes and moves. The **content** is the function of the action, in this case getting the clothes on the body.

Form and content are useful concepts. Separating out *why* we do something from *how* we do it, sharpens senses and clarifies intentions.

It will serve us throughout the training to look at form and content as if they were separate components of action. But, in reality, they're not. One informs the other and cannot exist in isolation.

> *Here's an example: Curl your fingers. The time, space, shape of the action of curling your fingers is the form; the intention of the action of curling your fingers is the content. How did you do it? Fast? Hard? Slow? Gently? Did you grab for something? Did you crush something? Say you slowly crushed a piece of paper by winding your fingers down into each other. The slow winding of your fingers is the form, the intention to crush the paper is the content. In action, one can't exist without the other. Together, they produce meaning.*

1B. Walk/Run/Freeze to Freeze in Same Scene

• Everybody, walk. A bit faster. Accelerate a bit more. Wide open strides. Breathe. Sometimes follow somebody. Go where they're going, walk as they walk. Frequently change directions. Avoid walking in a circle. Keep the pace up. Open strides. Stay focused on your breathing. Continue to watch your breath. Notice where everybody is and where everybody is walking. See yourself in the context of everyone in the room. Keep the pace up. From time to time, run. Run fast. You're either walking fast, or you're running fast. Sometimes follow somebody.

● And, now, from time to time, freeze, stopping all movement at once. Your whole body—your hands, your face, even your eyes—still. Hold your energy in that stillness. From time to time follow somebody. Freeze as they freeze. Eliminate the walking, so you're either running fast or you're still, absolutely still. The next time you freeze, freeze in a very dramatic, even melodramatic, posture and expression. Don't plan it. Impulsively leap into unknown territory. Pretend you're passionate, mad, emotionally haphazard. Be a demon. Sometimes follow somebody. Freeze as they freeze. Run as they run. Sometimes freeze in reaction to someone else's freeze, their shape, their condition. Move into their scene.

● Everyone run at the same time, freeze at the same time, and be in the same scene. Again. Again. Be in the same scene. Be sure to play different roles. Again, another scene. Darker. Be wild.

Students are looking at everyday activities: simple forms of walking, running and standing still. But they're operating in the context of a group, extending their awareness of time and space. They're observing each other specifically for shape, feeling, and intention of action. They're entering into **ensemble mind**.

Ensemble

Ensemble refers to a group of people who collectively and simultaneously construct theater work wherein each of them is considered only in relation to the whole. There are different kinds of ensembles. An Action Theater ensemble improvises theater collaboratively with no script, no director, no choreography. The individuals serve the collaborative intention. Who leads and who follows is irrelevant, and changes continually depending on the material presented. The group is single-minded, one organism.

Imagine a group of pelicans flying together in a "V." The members of an ensemble are like the individual birds. As the pelicans create their "V" in flight, so do the ensemble members create their scene of action.

The pelicans don't think, "Now, I'm making a 'V'," and the performers don't think, "Now, I'm making a scene." Both respond to their moment to moment experience relative to their intention. Both get the job done. Both are aware of their environment: sensing, discovering, relaying information, while at the same time, adapting to changes from within the group.

Ensemble work reflects how performers interact with their environment and each other. In an ensemble, performers constantly pass cues back and forth. To see and hear these cues, the performers require clear attention, freed of personal needs or wants.

They must:

1: Notice what the others are doing.

2: Believe what the others are doing is real.

3: Let the others' reality become their context.

4: Act from inside the context.

Inevitably, patterns enacted in ensemble are repeated outside the studio and visa versa. How aware are we of the spaces we inhabit? The other people in it? How does it feel to be moving closely with a group of people? How flexible can we be in changing places as follower and leader? Can we free ourselves from distracting judgments and preferences?

As the work evolves in the course of these twenty days, students change the way they relate to their internal voices. What was denied becomes acceptable and demons become creative resources. Condemning beliefs turn out to be negotiable—or, at least, intriguing limitations that transform into intricacies.

Form

When we per*form* an action, how we configure its content in time and space molds its meaning. Imagine all the different ways "I love you" might be spoken and all the corresponding meanings. If we were to analyze each "I love you" to see why they're distinct, then we'd have to talk about the timing of the words, volume, pitch and inflection of the voice, as well as the relationship between sound and breath. These are all elements of form that help define the action of saying, "I love you." **Form** defines action and effects meaning.

In Action Theater, we isolate four elements of **form: time, space, shape** and **dynamics**. We explore and experiment with them. By doing so, we expand awareness and open up our choices of expression.

Time

Timing refers to the relationship between one moment of change and the next. We must be aware of time, of now, otherwise our actions may not be relevant. With practice, we develop the ability to recognize and differentiate between moments. The inability to stay present in time is devastating; the inability to be with change is deadening. Here's a story.

One afternoon a family is out boating on a bay. The boat runs out of gas and drifts out to the mouth of the bay where the breakers are enormous. The boat overturns and the family is scattered in the water. Each person responds to the situation differently: one man clings to the capsized boat, terrorized; another swims desperately, trying to keep warm; the woman believes that the wreck is pre-destined and bargains with the sea for her life. None of these people consciously stay within time, within their changing environment. But the young boy who is with them does: he gives all of his attention to the way one moment follows the next. He learns how each moment contains clues for the next. He keeps his eye on the swell and swirlings around him and calls out directions to the others. Dive. Breathe. Float. Swim. Dive. Breathe. Because the boy stays in time, the family survives until the ocean releases them.

Personal agendas, and the resulting loss of awareness, described above, prevent us from living in the present. We allow beliefs to govern our actions, rather than our experience of the constant flow of change.

As our awareness of timing develops, we discover that each present moment holds everything we need to meet the next. In this flow of changing phenomena, we see that all the old moments have aided our delivery to this one, one moment falling out of another. There's no longer any thing as a false move.

We examine the timing of an action in two ways: **speed** and **duration**. Speed refers to the rate of change of an action. Duration refers to the time period an action lasts, from start to end, before it closes, or is interrupted by another action of differing form and/or content.

The following exercises invite students to make conscious choices about the speed and duration of two actions—movement and speech—in time. They work in partners. They must not only be aware of how their material exists in time, but how their time choices relate/respond to their partner's, too. They learn that movement and stillness, silence and sound live inside of time. No distinction exists between one person's movement and another's, only between movement and no movement.

1C. Move Same Time/Freeze Same Time

• Everybody, take a partner. Stand face-to-face. One Rule: Move at the same time and stop moving at the same time. You are always moving in sync. You can be moving in different ways. You can be moving at different speeds. You can be moving with different qualities. But your intention is to start at the same time and stop at the same time. Hold the stillness for varying lengths of time. Sometimes be still for a moment, sometimes be still for many moments. Be erratic.

1D. Move at Different Times

• Stand face-to-face with your partner. One of you is A, the other is B. A moves and continues moving until B interrupts with movement. A stops and B moves until A interrupts, and so on. Fill your movements so that they're not empty forms, but your forms have intention to them. In other words, your movements reflect your current state of mind. If nothing is going on, pretend there is.

◗ •

Basic timing exercises give students something very specific to watch: *when* they do something, *when* they don't, *when* they start, and *when* they stop. Their every move must be conscious. Students realize they have choice. They start and they stop. They change. They determine their experience.

Self-consciousness may come and go throughout the training. Because of new and unusual perspectives on one's behavior, students often worry and inhibit expression. They start to think about "right" or "wrong" actions; they begin to think before they act. This analytical and planning frame of mind eventually loses its prominence. As learning progresses, old patterns no longer fit. Observing behavior stops being an assignment and becomes second nature, a matter of awareness.

"If nothing is going on, pretend there is." "Be in the nothing." Both of these directions are useful. The former awakens the ability to fantasize; the latter sanctifies the mundane, the dishonored. Everything is mind, whether theater or life. Differentiating between interesting and dull, mundane and profound, worthy and unworthy, drains the heart, kills the spirit, and paralyzes the body. Just go for the details.

In the last exercise of the day, we bring our attention to speech. We start to talk. We talk in front of an audience.

◗ •

1E. Performance Score: Autobiographies

• Four people, sit facing the rest of the group. Take turns speaking autobiographically about your "real" life. Be factual. Tell us where you grew up, what your family was like, your schooling, etc. Only one of you speaks at a time and continues until interrupted. Just as we did earlier today, have the interruptions be erratic, so that the monologues vary in length. In other words, you might interrupt each other very quickly, or you might allow, from time to time, someone to speak a bit longer. As you describe the events or conditions of your life, play with the form of your monologues, change the sounds of your words. Speak from an attitude or feeling that is different from the way you would normally speak. Not necessarily opposite, just different.

Language

Most of us go through our daily lives unaware of how we do what we do. For example, our speech is probably locked into a pattern that we don't even recognize; it has a particular rhythm, inflection, tone. We've never really listened to our voices. As a result, when we hear ourselves on a tape recorder we're surprised.

Autobiographies introduces students to a new way of listening to themselves, others, and themselves in connection with others. They listen *from inside and outside* of the sound. There's no trick to it. All that's required is to turn attention toward the flow of sound: the mouth and ear experience.

Students collaborate, listening and relating through what they hear in timing, tone and attitude. What they hear affects what they do and what they do affects what they hear. Pieces of their stories intersperse with pieces of others'. Affected by what they hear from others in the group, students recast the emotional value of their own autobiographies. Their investment in who they are and what they're talking about changes. They might speak with sensuality about the death of a baby brother, with military cadence about the breaking of bones, or with a particular glee about the pressing urgency of a job.

Students are learning to hear **form** (how they speak) separate from, yet linked, to **content** (what they say). They start to see that any emotional reaction to phenomena is self-created and can be changed. This realization leads to flexibility in how they interpret occurrences in their lives, much less on stage. It also points to the infinite possibilities of meaning.

Each session ends with a score. A score is a performance structure, and is different from an exercise. An exercise focuses inward and is specifically designed to develop a skill. In an exercise, the participants are not consciously sharing their event with an audience. They're not directing their expression to anyone other than to a partner. A score, on the other hand, encompasses the skills practiced in exercises and plays them *out* for an audience.

Day One has introduced students to four fundamentals of Action Theater: 1) **form**; 2) **ensemble**; 3) **timing**; and 4) **language**. In exercises that work with the first three components, students take simple steps. Attention returns to everyday activities, awareness of others in the same environment and the details of behavior. As the month proceeds, the exercises build upon these primary concepts and point toward a sophisticated practice. The last exercise, **Autobiographies**, is a complex exercise requiring a practiced skill. It's introduced on the first day as a glimpse of the multi-dimensional material yet to come.

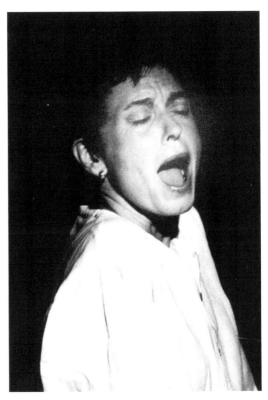

The Body's Voice

2A. Breath Circle
2B. Sounder/Mover
2C. All at Once: Sound and Movement
2D. Sound and Movement Diagonal
2E. Performance Score: Sound and Movement Solo

How do we express ourselves?
What possibilities do we have?
We can move, speak, and make sounds.
We can do these one at a time,
or we can combine them.
Most of the time we don't choose.
Whatever happens, happens.

In the present moment, we have the capacity to simultaneously notice vast amounts of information from the body's senses and the mind's activities of memory, thought and imagination. But our ability to be aware of and integrate this information needs to be developed. It's a muscle to be exercised. One way we do this is by examining the way we express ourselves, through action—movement, vocal sounds and speech.

Expression is both the interpretation of experience and experience itself. Suppose we have an idea that we want to communicate and we choose language as our vehicle. Think of all the ways language can be formed to express that idea. Each form is a living experience and through its moments, throws a different light on the original idea.

In the same way, movement or vocalization may draw from the same idea, but each moment of action determines the next, thereby creating its own experience.

Voice, body and language are different vocabularies. When we operate through one of these modes, we perceive through its vocabulary. This accesses different information. Each mode transmits through its capabilities and is framed by its limitations. What can be said with language, can't necessarily be said with movement, and vice versa. Depending on what realm of the psyche we're inhabiting, movement, sound or language may be the most appropriate choice.

What we call **sound and movement** is when a physical and vocal action arise simultaneously. Most of the time they don't. There are rare occasions when movement and voice are tied to each other: we simultaneously jump and scream at being surprised, we sneeze and our body contracts, we stretch and moan when we wake up in the morning.

Breath

To prepare for consciously joining the voice and movement, we begin with the breath.

> *Sometimes, I watch my chattering mind (the judgmental mind, the mind that berates, criticizes, or labels). Sometimes, I give my mind something to focus on that isn't chattering. I watch breath. Breath always goes on. I don't have to make it happen, or pick it up from anywhere, or borrow it from anybody. Breath is right here.*

2A. Breath Circle

• Stand in a circle. Focus on your breath. The air comes in, bounces out, pauses. Watch that. Observe your breath for a few minutes. Now, play with reordering the timing and dynamic, or power, of your breath: when and how it comes in, bounces out, and the duration of the pause. Mess it up. Disrupt its regularity.

• Now, let's start a game. Everyone stand in the large circle and breathe normally. At some point, any one of you can step inside the large circle and form an inner circle. The first person that goes in sets up a breath pattern using air sound, aspirant sounds. No voice. Continue that pattern for as long as you are in the inner circle. Anybody can join the inner circle by either setting up a companion pattern, or by mirroring a pattern that's already there. It's possible that everyone will be in the inner circle at the same time, either doing the same breath pattern or complementary ones. You can go in and out of the inner circle at any time, but every time you enter it, you must start a new pattern and keep it until you leave. After, maybe, ten minutes we add voice. All the rules stay the same.

Constantly, we practice a subtle sound and movement exercise by breathing. Our lungs expand with each inhalation, rib cages widen, bellies round, shoulder girdles float a little higher. If we listen, we hear a tiny wind enter. As it exits with a different sound, everything settles. We often forget this vital connection between sound and movement.

The Breath Circle has prepared us for the next exercise, which is a freer sound and movement exploration.

2B. Sounder/Mover

• In partners, one of you is the sounder, and the other is the mover.

• Sounder, focus inward. This is your journey. Don't focus on your mover. You don't even have to look at your partner. Concentrate. Listen to your voice and the passion it inspires.

• Start with any sound, an impulsive sound. Open your mouth and let something come out. Follow what you hear without judgment. Respond to whatever feelings or mind states come into your awareness. Avoid, for now, singing or rhythmic patterns.

• Mover, you're movement reflects exactly what it is that you hear; you're translating the sounds into movement. If that sound has a body, you are moving the way that body would move. If the sound pauses, you pause. If the sound speeds up, you speed up. If the sound becomes harsh, you get harsh. If the sound is soft, soften. Through you, the sound becomes movement.

• When I say, "Stop," have a little chat with your partner. Talk about how it worked for both of you, what you liked, felt comfortable with, sailed with, where you got bogged down, how you handled that, what you could have done to get out of a jam or into one, what you want to be aware of the next time you repeat this exercise.

• Repeat the exercise, this time reversing roles.

Often after partnering exercises, students are instructed to talk to each other about their experiences. Together, they develop a discriminating perspective, share a way of seeing things and talking about them. They tell each other what they noticed about each other's actions, how they experienced them. Students are directed to *not* tell each other what they would have liked to have seen or what they think the other *should* do.

> *Before I started identifying birds with binoculars and bird books, I was a generic observer. I saw red bird, blue bird, maybe big yellow bird with black legs. Identifying birds aroused my curiosity. I began to look for detail, not just so I could name species but because I could see more wonder, detail. I developed a language, a discriminating perspective. Other birders and I detailed our sightings to each other. Then, I could see even more detail.*

Rhythm

One of our tasks in this training is to develop the body as a finely tuned instrument of expression. One aspect of this is the ability to consciously move or gesture while speaking. Too often, while speaking the body slips into regular timing, movement weakens and dies out, reduces to stillness, or becomes habitual and lacks meaning. Irregular timing insists that students stay present in their body, that they make relevant choices as to when they execute the action, how long they pause between actions, and how long each action lasts. (Except for occasional exercises later in the training, irregular timing is always required.)

The sounders were directed to investigate non-rhythmic, non-musical, irregular sounds. For instance, saying, "BA," in rhythmic time would look like this: "BA BA BA BA." In non-rhythmic time, it could look like this: "BA BABA BA BA BA BA   BA   BA BA BA BA BABABA   BA," with no pattern repeating itself.

> *Try this: Clap at regular intervals for a few minutes. Now, clap at irregular intervals. How do you experience the difference? Now, simultaneously, tell a story while you clap irregularly. Can you do it? It's difficult. It takes practice. Your attention is split: the clapping and the story. If, on the other hand, you clapped at regular intervals, you wouldn't have to focus on the clapping at all. You could get into a groove and not even have to think about it. But, the action of clapping would lose its independent voice, becoming background for the story.*

Spontaneity

Where does our material come from? The interaction of sensation, imagination and memory.

Another goal of this training is to access all co-existing realms of experience, even those our language can't describe—the states that can't be named, that at best, we call "states of spirit."

When we act from an open mind, with the various realms accessible, and express ourselves through body, voice or language, we're spontaneous. We can travel through primal and emotional states, states of cognition and exaltation, and dream or fantasy states that order phenomena in extra-ordinary ways.

⌣ •

2C. All at Once: Sound and Movement

• Start very simply, a simple movement with your hand, your head, or one leg. Sound the gesture as you do it. Make the sound and the movement occur simultaneously, exist for the same amount of time, be of the same texture and quality. For instance, closing your right hand: as you close your right hand, make a vocal sound that's of the same time duration and movement quality. Let one sound and movement lead you to another, and so on. Vary your speeds and qualities. Work with this on your own for a few minutes. Stay focused on your inner experience. Screen out the activities of the others around you.

⌣ •

As we take apart and examine forms of expression, be it movement, sound or speech, we become more aware of ourselves in relation to our experience. Clearly, we are *not* our experience. We're the consciousness that witnesses that process. We're not our feelings. Feelings, emotions, and thoughts pass through us. When we laugh, we're not laughter, we're experiencing laughter; we're aware of it: we hear it and feel it. Once we become aware of ourselves laughing, we notice a space between our awareness and the laughter—between the one who is doing and the action that's being done. It's from this perspective, that we're able to play with the sound of laughter, and even the feel of it.

The awareness that our every action is a construct of some constellation of influences can be devastating at first. We don't know what's ours, and what's been handed down to us. We don't know who we are. Eventually, this understanding frees us. We let go of all that we've been holding and realize that we never had anything anyway.

When we're improvising, personal material may occasionally surface. We have a choice—whether to allow the images or feelings to be expressed or to push them back into the shadows of the psyche. If it's fear that causes us to repress this material, we're constantly working under

this limitation. This affects everything we do. We're always on guard. If, on the other hand, we hold these images and feelings, with curiosity and an understanding that they're only images and feelings, and we still choose not to express the image or feeling because of their appropriateness to the moment, we're free to move along. In other words, we detach from what we call our own, what's preciously ours. Opportunities are infinite once we can freely explore our psyches. The overwhelming panic that we have nothing to say becomes panic to play with. The "unacceptable" flaw which we keep hidden is already familiar. The grace that we envy in others is available to us. There is no "mine" and no "yours."

2D. Sound and Movement Dialogue

• Stand in a diagonal line across the floor, facing the same direction, everybody equidistant from each other, so that you're looking at the back of the person in front of you (except for the first person).

• The first person turns around to the person behind—this is all done quickly—and presents a sound and movement action. Clear form, clear intention. The second person mirrors that action, form and content, and then turns to the person behind them (3rd person) and does another sound and movement for that person. That third person mirrors the second person's sound and movement, turns, and responds with a sound and movement action for the next person. And we do this up and down the line.

• Get faster. Let go. Get faster to let go. Actions become like a wave, up and down the line, and nobody's thinking. Everybody's mirroring, responding, mirroring, responding. Faster, faster, smooth it out, faster, don't think, respond. Pretend you're wild, erratic, nuts, impulsive, out of control. Faster, faster, faster, get it, give it, get it, give it, faster.

The mirroring and responding of this exercise demands that students free themselves from any pre-conceived plans or notions. Increasingly higher speeds, and front-to-back change, turn each student into a carrier, an electron. There's no time to create a new path, there's only time to keep the current flowing. Because of the speed, students' responses tend to move into areas and territories they haven't previously let themselves explore. But even the new and exciting encounter can't be indulged in, it must be embraced once and let go.

2E. Performance Score: Sound and Movement Solo

• Each of you will take a turn on the floor alone for two minutes. This a time for you to practice sound and movement action without the disturbance of others around you. Let one action cue the next. Stay inside yourself. Follow your inspiration. You're not working for the audience. This is your time. Breathe. The rest of us will be your audience. We will pass a watch, so that we can take turns timing each other.

Holding one's concentration with oneself during an improvisation, while holding the pressures of performance, is important. It takes practice. In these early days of the training, students have the opportunity to notice what arises when they're in front of the others. As they become comfortable with this experience, they can use that material as resource for building imagery.

In the training, we spend the majority of our time together exploring the exercises, rather than verbally talking about the work. This learning occurs *in the doing*. To analyze would be to render students passive when the most important lessons will be learned while active. Nothing is being asked of students that is not inherent to their physical and mental capabilities. In that sense, all we need to know, we already know. In the act of doing, we remember that.

When we talk about "choices" during an improvisation we don't mean that before taking any action we must weigh all of our possibilities and, then, by educated judgment choose the most enlightened course of expression. Choice is a split second response to freedom. We can only be free when we're not afraid of fear. Freedom is the absence of fear of fear. When we can play with our fears—fear of exposure, fear of not being good enough, fear of reprisal, we approach the path of freedom. Fear of fear is the cork that bottles the body and imagination. When the cork is popped, choice exists.

Voice and movement are often separate. Day Two helps develop skill and consciousness in all areas at once. Students balance their attention between what's coming out of their mouths and what's going through their bodies. They move toward integrating these two, and realizing more clearly when they should be separate.

Day Three

A Way to Proceed:
Body, Imagination, Memory

3A. Falling Leaves/Rock with Movement, Sound and Dialogue
3B. Shape Alphabet
3C. Shape/Shape/Reshape
3D. Director/Actor: Shift with Movement, Sound and Language
3E. Performance Score: Two Up/Two Down

The headlights coming toward me are bright. Dropping down the hill, I see the trailing red snake tail lights. My eyes squint. I can feel my face crumbling. My skin is dry. Relax! I raise my spine and stretch it out. The wipers tap out a tack-a-shooshoo-tack rhythm. The air is thick and wet. Maybe there'll be a small audience tonight. It's too wet and cold to go out. My body collapses and my breath speeds up, chest is tight. Park. Turn the key and be quiet. Sit. Don't go in yet. Listen to the rain. OK, go in. Pull the door handle. It's hard and cold. Twist around, get out of the car. Pull the coat up and walk. Sigh. I'm in the theater and it's comforting, familiar, and quiet. Breathe. Audience chatters muffled words and laughter. I feel a pulse. It's mine and fast. There's a black curtain between the stage and me. Pace to the window, then to the curtain, then to the window, and to the curtain again. My tongue glides over my lips. They're dry and my chest is tight. I pull apart the curtain and walk toward a spot on stage. My heart is fast. Breathe. Breathe and relax. Be still. Hold still. Stay still. Don't rush. My mouth and lips draw back. My mouth opens.

Our mind shifts its attention from object to object in erratic and irreverent ways. We can move from thought to feeling to imagining to remembering to sound to thought to taste to vision to thought and on and on. The less we control and inhibit this movement and the more we watch and listen, the freer our minds are to play with this vast assortment.

On the other hand, we can worry, think, conjure, create, devise, imagine or cook up what we're going to do, say, or be next. While we're busy doing this, we're missing out on the present moment. We aren't in our bodies, i.e., we're no longer aware of the information coming in through our senses. Our attention is on the future. When we reach the future, the actions thought up in the past are no longer relevant. While we were spending time thinking, our environment changed. Our context is different.

Thinking is too slow. When we're thinking about the future moment, we're thinking about what's next. "Next" is a thought. Whatever we think up lacks freshness. When we're thinking—as opposed to listening to ourselves with less attachment and staying with each moment—we never get beyond ourselves and the familiar.

Fresh material is a surprise response to the interaction between body, imagination and memory. There's a direct link between the three. It's kind of a body-heart-head thing. If my attention is on the sensations of my body, that awareness may elicit memories, feeling and imagination. It all happens at once, not up or down, no particular starting point.

This practice of Action Theater offers a way to proceed. It is a visceral lead to linking body, imagination and memory; to opening up to fresh experience and expression.

Shift, Transform, Develop

Experience evolves. In the natural world, change occurs continuously. Change occurs at varying speeds from lightning fast to slow browning of leaves. Sometimes change strikes abruptly without warning. Sometimes, incrementally, step by step. And sometimes, change transpires so slowly that we don't see the change at all.

Since we're part of the natural world we are, also, continuously changing. We change our minds, what we're doing and how we're feeling. We might change in an instant, **shift** from one state or condition to another. It's not always apparent why. But there's always an inner motivation, a hidden bridge that ties one experience to another.

When we change gradually, step by step, or evolve, we **transform.** It's apparent how one state or condition moves into another.

It might appear that we aren't changing at all. In such cases, change proceeds subtly, under the surface. During this type of change, we engage with the action we are in, we **develop** it.

Within this system, there are no other options. All events, actions, and situations either **shift, transform** or **develop.**

> *Imagine a situation where all three modes of change occur at the same time. For instance, I am talking on the telephone while cooking oatmeal on the stove. During the course of the conversation, my feelings gradually change due to what I'm hearing. I move from contentment to curiosity to anger to understanding to contentment, step by step* (**transform**). *The oatmeal gets too hot and threatens to burn. I stir more rapidly* (**transform**), *and, in panic, yank the pot from the stove* (**shift**). *All this while, I remain talking on the telephone* (**develop**).

Shifting, transforming and **developing** are ways to proceed that respond to awareness rather than thought. All are strategies of change.

Modes of change:

Shift	stop the action and do something else.
Transform	change the action incrementally until it becomes something else.
Develop	continue the action.

3A. Falling Leaves with Movement, Sound and Dialogue

With Movement

• Stand somewhere in the room. Close your eyes. Watch your breath. Place your attention somewhere in your body that specifically senses breath: the base of your nose, diaphragm or abdomen. Observe the experience of the breath as it comes in and goes out. Watch the pause between each breath.

• Every five or six minutes, I'm going to call out words to you that describe natural phenomena. These phenomena "move" in a particular way. Their timing, how they travel through space, their weight, shape and dynamic are peculiar to them. As you imagine each phenomenon, explore movement that reflects the these qualities. Don't pantomime, or act out, or pretend that you are the phenomenon itself. Explore motion within the movement quality the image evokes.

Electricity

Falling leaves.
Electricity.
Rock.
Lightning.
Mud.
Thunder.
Gentle breezes.

• As you are moving, allow whatever feelings, thoughts, attitudes or states of mind entering your awareness to affect what you are doing; the tension of your body, the expression on your face, the gaze of your eyes may change. Don't hold onto anything or make a story but stay on one thing long enough to define it for yourself. Let your imagination respond freely to your body's actions.

Rock.
Falling leaves.
Whirlpool.
Lightning.
Thunder.
Tornado.
Electricity.
Rock.
Electricity.
Rock.
Falling leaves.
Rock.
Electricity.
Mud.

Mud

• In the next few moments, associate with one, or two, people in the room and continue to explore the qualities you've been investigating in relation to one another. You may both be moving with the same qualities, or different ones. Respond to your own behavior and to your partner's behavior as well.

With Sound
• Again, I will call out these nouns. But, now, explore sound and movement. The kinetic quality you associate with these images is expressed physically and vocally. Remember, every sound you make must be connected to movement and every movement is connected to sound. Otherwise, be still and silent.

With Dialogue
• Stand facing a partner. Again, I will call out

Falling Leaves

Rock

Thunder

these nouns. When you hear them, assume the quality of energy in your body that these words suggest. Don't do any movement. Stand fairly still. Let these energies affect your voice, feelings, attitudes and even the content of your language. Have a dialogue with your partner. As you hear me say each new noun, shift to the appropriate energy while continuing the content.

Falling Leaves is a **shift** exercise. Students change abruptly from one psycho-physical state to another. This is not pantomime. To pantomime a rock, one might pretend to be something other than oneself. In **Falling Leaves/Rock**, students go inside themselves to find the un-ordinary states of body-mind, rather than going outside themselves to find the ordinary. An inner quality of "rock" can manifest in a variety of ways: one can walk down the street with looseness of a pebble in a stream; respond to a barroom seduction with a hard, cold, impenetrable rock-like demeanor; discuss the pros and cons of waging war with an ancient well-worn wisdom. One might eat soup in time with leaves falling, talk about last night's sleep in thunder voice or play with a child as electric energy.

At first, as students embody these energies, predictable feelings or states of mind arise. Thunder elicits loud rage; electricity, erratic madness; leaves falling, swaying peacefulness; mud, thick sensuality; lightning, directed aggression; etc. As students repeatedly play in these energies, the mind states released from each form become less predictable and more surprising, less nameable and more knowable.

Later in the training, practiced students may pretend that they are in fact a "rock." But at that point, they're prepared to approach the ordinary with extra-ordinary attention. Rather than hearing "rock" as a limitation, they explore rock with a mind open to sensation, feelings and imagination. "Rockness" becomes an avenue into hidden personal realms, the "rockness" living inside.

Who Are We?

One of Action Theater's objectives is to detail perception by expanding awareness:

- of the energy and tension of the body
- of feeling and imagination's link to the body
- of ourselves from the inside out

We don't use the word "character" in Action Theater. Sometimes we say "entity" or "physical presence." Or we say "being." "Character" produces stereotypes. It asks us to be somebody other than who we are. A somebody that can be described, "a cranky judge," "a bored wife," "a hard-talking waitress." Instead, we manifest a vast array of entities, parts of ourselves that are, up until then, hidden in our psyches. We build upon our uncovered components to create "beings" who are whole and complete.

The detailed perception we acquire through practice is reflected by precise expression. In order to express ourselves in detail, we must know and control our body and mind. If we are still and empty, we become a blank canvas on which to project the nature of our psyches.

The following exercises lead students toward physical awareness, a first step toward an expressive body.

3B. Shape Alphabet

• I'm going to call out the letters of the alphabet, A through Z. As you hear each letter, you'll only have two or three seconds to form it with your body. As much as possible, exactly create the shape of the letter.

A B C D E F G H I J K L M N O P Q R S T U V W X Y Z

• Now, take a partner. Again, I'm going to call out the letters of the alphabet, and with your partner, without talking, and especially without laughing, form the letters together. Both of your bodies should form one letter. Concentrate!

A B C D E F G H I J K L M N O P Q R S T U V W X Y Z

Shape

How do we know our body? As an instrument to perform daily tasks, such as picking up things, moving from place to place, throwing, kicking and squeezing? As a tender or tough wrapper protecting what needs to be nourished, fed, covered up, rested, exercised and, on occasion, medicated or repaired? As a source of information, full of stories, mysteries and ancient truths? Do we know our body as an instrument of communication? How aware are we of what it is saying? Do we know its capability for infinite design and meaning? Probably not.

Shape Alphabet encourages students to see themselves from the outside, externally. It helps them determine if their body shape reflects their intention (in this case, making each letter). Also, if the shape they pick relates to their environment—their partner's shape. Watching others and themselves, through trial and error, trains the performer's inner eye. Students learn to make images that precisely fit their experience. The small turn of a finger, tilt of the head, inversion of the foot, or the glance of the eyes can completely alter the meaning of a shape. This kind of visual acuity, creating image, is a basic performance skill.

> performer or not
> quiet body leads to quiet mind
> quiet mind leads to awareness
> —unobstructed—
> all things equal

3C. Shape/Shape/Reshape

• Get a new partner.

• A makes a shape, any shape. B makes a different shape and places it in relation to A's shape. Then A steps out of his/her shape and reshapes in relation to B's shape. Then B steps out and reshapes in relation to A's shape.

• Do this slowly and smoothly so that you step out of one shape and mold into the next shape without stopping, going into neutral, thinking, deciding, planning or creating. Don't touch each other. Don't put weight on each other, because then your partner won't be able to change shape.

• As you do this, I'm going to suggest directions, from time to time. Design your shapes accordingly.

Shape/Shape/Reshape

Spacious
Constricted, tight
Angular, twisted, knotted
Circular, round, arched
Complex, detailed

• Inhabit your shapes. Fill them with feeling or attitude. Begin to speed up. Vary the quality of your shapes—work within the same quality as your partner, or sometimes be different. Vary your timing. Increase your speed until you are moving percussively from shape to shape, responding impulsively to each other's shapes and meanings.

• We'll repeat a portion of this exercise with one half of the group watching the other.

No Touch

Improvisation practice confronts "aloneness" and all of its conditions. For the first two weeks of the training, students are asked to avoid making physical contact during the exercises. Touching, pushing, pulling, bending, re-arranging, lifting, leaning on, scratching, caressing, tickling, massaging each other are all actions that direct attention away from the toucher and onto the touched.

When improvising and feeling lost or stuck, grabbing somebody else seems like a life saving gesture, like grabbing a log while drowning. A student may clutch another in order to hold onto somebody or something familiar, or resort to touch in order to project an unconscious inner experience onto another. For example, if a student feels pressured to do something, she might turn around and pass that pressure on to someone else by literally pressing on them.

Later, once students can confidently express their moment to moment experience, the "No Touching" restriction is removed. As a result, touch takes on a different meaning. Emphasis is put on **how** the touch is executed and its inner aspects. It is in the detailed quality of the action, as

well as the kind of action, that meaning is created, e.g., a push can be executed powerfully and percussively indicating aggression, or slowly and softly indicating love.

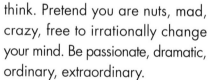

3D. Director/Actor: Shift with Movement, Sound and Language

• In partners. One of you is "Director," one of you is "Actor." Director, you can say one word only, and that word is "Shift."

• Actor, when you hear the word shift, you change your mind, stop doing what you're doing and do something else that is immediately relevant, yet

contrasts with what you just were doing. If what you were just doing was upright, stationary and slow, your next form might be travelling and jerky, and low to the floor. This shift happens abruptly, a sudden switch. When you hear the word, "Shift," stay inside yourself and respond to whatever you are aware of at that moment: the feeling you currently have, something you see, hear, touch, fantasize or

think. Pretend you are nuts, mad, crazy, free to irrationally change your mind. Be passionate, dramatic, ordinary, extraordinary.

• Director, play with your timing. You can say, "Shift," sooner, you can say, "Shift," later. Let the person stay in their material for longer periods, and/or make them change rapidly and irregularly.

• When you have completed this

exercise, have a chat with each other. Director, tell the actor how you experienced her range of feeling and action. Was there contrast? Was the actor "connecting" to what she was doing?

• Repeat this exercise, changing roles.

• Change partners and repeat this sequence, but now, shift with sound and movement. Every time the actor hears her director say, "Shift," she should respond to whatever comes into her awareness at that moment. She expresses that response with sound and movement.

• Again, have a discussion and reverse roles.

• Change partners again and repeat the sequence with monologues. For now, don't concern yourself with movement, just speak. When you hear "Shift," respond to whatever comes into your awareness. Stay in your body, your source of energy and information.

• Remember, you're out of your mind.

◞ •

The director in this exercise is not a care-taker. Her job is not to pull the actor out of tough situations. Instead, the director facilitates the "stretching" of the actor, even if that means the actor squirming uncomfortably. Squirming is as okay as anything else.

Unfortunately, a person can get lost in squirming. She can lose awareness, and judgment without knowing she's squirming or she judges squirming as "bad." Then, self-recrimination sets in.

Converting squirming (unintentional movement), from a bad, uncomfortable action into simply another action, without thoughts

attached, takes practice. Awareness has to be tuned. Sensations in all parts of the mind and body need to be noted: what does squirming feel like? how does it move? breathe? what's its timing, tension? With awareness, there's no more squirming, just a particular condition that can't even be called anything. Unnameable yet knowable.

The student may get frustrated with a rapid firing of the "Shift" direction. The opportunity to go with what's happening presents itself again and again. If frustrated or under duress, the student may finally let go, give up and relax into her wildness.

If the director allows the performer to stay with a reality for a long time, the same thing may happen. The performer may feel frustrated. Or again, under the duress of having to stick with something, the performer may relax into the sensations, feelings, and actions of that something. Again and again, opportunity presents itself. Focus, stay in the body of experience.

Listening

Say, "How are you?" Now, say, "How are you?" and listen to yourself. Can you create a score of the words with a line drawing? If a line drawn represents each word, would the melody and the timing look like this, − _ _, or this, − _ −, or this, _ _ −?

Say, "How are you?" with a different meaning. What does the line look like now?

The next time you talk on the telephone, have a pencil and paper ready. Notate the sound of the language as you receive it. Distance yourself from the content so that you can **listen** to the words as sounds. (The content of words often interferes with listening.) Score the language as you hear it. Each word may give a rise, or a drop, or a stutter.

Awareness comes with a quiet mind and body. Only a quiet mind listens. Only a quiet mind is free from impediments such as personal agendas, preferences, criticisms, ideas, opinions and thinking ahead. Just as a quiet mind listens, listening quiets the mind.

3E. Performance Score: Two Up/Two Down

• Two people sit in the chairs facing the audience, and two other people stand up behind them. The two people sitting on the chairs will initiate material. The two people standing up will echo.

• One seated person will start by saying a line, a short sentence or phrase. The other three will then repeat that line and play with it musically. The line has to be repeated with exactly the same intonation and intention as given, but the music builds with timing and delivery. Then, another line is offered by either one of the initiators. Each one of these lines must be radically different from one another: the voice quality, volume, pitch, speed, content. The initiators may each say up to three lines.

• The people standing above can only echo the lines that they've heard. The initiators can echo each other's line, as well as, their own.

• All of you collaborate on the sound composition. Listen to each other. In a sense, you're talking to each other. Hear the lines in relation to each other, both the sound and content. Play with it.

• Reverse roles. The two sitting, stand. The two standing, sit.

Here students focus on the sound patterns of their language. No fancy technique is needed. No perfected voice. No years of training. They have all the equipment they need: ears, mouths, and willingness. They interact like jazz musicians composing a score from the sounds of everyday language.

When we were children, we changed our minds on a dime. We were experts on change and great **shifters**. We'd cry one minute and laugh the next. We'd take seriously what was or wasn't serious. We "listened" because there wasn't anything else on our minds. We believed in what we were doing, and we dropped it without a thought if something else took our attention. That's what **shift** is all about.

Two Up/Two Down

Composition

4A. Lay/Sit/Stand
4B. Walk on Whispered "Ah"
4C. Focus In/Eyes Out
4D. Mirroring
4E. Accumulation, One Leader
4F. Performance Score: Accumulation, All Leaders

She was moving very slowly. I could barely see any movement at all. Yet, from time to time, as I glanced at her, I saw her in slightly different postures. Then, she was crying. Later, she said it was because she was moving so slowly. She said she saw no images, no story, and was aware of only slowness and breath. Her mind was quiet for the first time.

We begin the fourth day by slowing down and allowing our attention to rest on hardly anything. The first task offers an opportunity to notice the activity of the mind.

~ •

4A. Lay/Sit/Stand

• Everyone, either lie down, sit, or stand and be very still. Focus on your breath. Watch the air as it comes in and bounces out. Watch the pause that follows each exhale. Feel that experience. Continue focusing on your breath while I describe the opening exercise.

• In the next few moments, begin moving as slowly and smoothly as possible. No pauses, jolts or jerks. As you move, pass through the simple postures of lying down, sitting, standing, and walking in any order. Move very, very slowly. Walking, sitting, lying down and standing. Ask yourself to move more slowly, and even slower than that. Pay attention to where you are. You have no place to go other than where you are. Move so slowly that you note every sensation coming into your awareness. Nothing evades your attention.

• As you're moving through these constantly changing postures, different states of mind may arise. Allow these states of mind, feelings, emotions to affect what you're doing: the energy in your body, expression on your face, and gaze of your eyes. Continue moving as slowly as you possibly can.

• From time to time, speed up a small section of the lying down, sitting, standing and walking action. Very fast. Percussive. Don't plan it. Pretend that someone else is directing you, someone else is making it happen. These fast movements are erratic, irregular: sometimes, a series of rapid movements: sometimes, a long period of slow movement before another rapid one appears.

• Gradually increase the amount of fast movements, and decrease the amount of slow ones. So, you will be either moving as fast as you possibly can or as slowly.

• Now begin to associate with someone in the room—a partner, someone near you—and continue to move in relation to one another. Respond to what they're doing, how they're doing it, their rate of speed, the shape they're making, the attitude or spirit they're expressing.

• Eliminate the slow movement. Now, you're either moving very fast, or you're still. You're directly communicating with each other. Lying down, sitting, standing and walking is your language. Only lying down, sitting, standing or walking. Nothing else.

• Don't try to be creative. No plans or choreography. Nothing fancy.

Creativity

"Being creative" is not something beyond us, nor do we have to become it. "Creative" is an idea that compartmentalizes and limits our experience. When we start thinking about being creative, we break from the present. Our bodies are in one place (present) and our minds are in another (future).

Another way to look at creativity is to say that it's not about being creative, but simply about being. "Being creative" implies being *other* than who you are, when actually creativity is being *more* of who you are.

We can find this by quieting down, relaxing, letting go of the future and simplifying our actions. What's the least you need to do to communicate exactly what you mean? Clear, spontaneous expression is not the result of how much you do, but rather, the quality of attention you give. Thus we ask the student to intentionally do very little and discover fullness in that smallness. Slow down their mind and pay attention to each moment of change. Adding more action won't compensate for lack of attention. Simplify. Bare the bone. Don't build with more action, build with more attention. Then, you'll be "creative."

Communication relies on intention and skill. I may want to communicate something to you but I don't have the skills for it. For example: I want you to know that I'm feeling sad, but I don't have the language or expression to transmit that information. Or, I get so wrapped up in my experience that I forget to notice whether you're listening and understanding what I'm saying. A lift of an eyebrow can be a powerful communication if one intends it to be so.

The quality of attention, of relaxed awareness, determines one's relationship to the changing aspects of experience. Whether performing improvisationally, playing a musical instrument, cooking, changing a diaper, or running a board meeting, creativity comes with attention.

Suppose attention can be measured in units, and altogether you have 100 of these units to work with. And suppose action can also be measured and you intend to perform 100 units of action. Units of action require units of attention in order to be clear and complete. The less individual actions you do, the more attention you can give to those actions. You have 100 actions to complete and only 100 units of attention to work with. How many units of attention per action? Well, obviously, you spread out the 100 units of attention evenly among the 100 actions. Every action then gets equal attention. But, suppose you have only one action to perform. You would apply your 100 units of attention to your one action. That's focus!

An example of redirecting attention is shown in **Walk on Whispered "Ah."** Students practice the "ah" sound focusing attention on the execution: listening, controlling and hearing the resonance of this most unincumbered sound.

4B. Walk on Whispered "Ah"

• Everybody walk briskly. Focus on your breath. Two steps with your inhale, two steps with your exhale. The air comes in, bounces out, and there's a pause. The next time you exhale, open your mouth, drop your jaw and exhale with a whispered "ah" sound. Inhale, then, exhale with a whispered "ah" sound, one for each step, "ah, ah." Let your mouth hang open. Open mouth, open "ah" sound.

• The next time you exhale, put more push behind the "ah" sound. This will give your voice more volume. Use your diaphragm.

• The next time you exhale, add a little voice. Stay easy, soft throat, relax. The air comes in, bounces out, small voice, "ah" sound, relaxed throat, and then a pause. Two steps for your inhalation, two steps for your exhalation with the "ah" sound. Two steps inhale, two steps exhale with the "ah" sound. Exhale. Inhale: step, step; exhale: "ah," "ah." Inhale: step, step. Exhale: "ah," "ah."

• Change the "ah" sound to "oh" sound.

• Do each of the vowels. Inhale, two steps, exhale, two steps, "oh," "oh." Inhale, two steps, exhale, two steps, "e," "e." Inhale, two steps, exhale, two steps, "u," "u." Relax your face, loosen the muscles, exaggerate the articulation. "A," "o," "e," "i," "u." Accelerate your steps, faster. Vowel on every step. "A," "o," "e," "i," "u," . . . "a," "o," "e," "i," "u," . . . "a," "o," "e," "i," "u."

Except for sporting events and occasional rage, many of us are afraid of being powerful or raising our voices. Yet, voice and all its complimentary energy is elemental to our existence. "Ah-ing" over and over again, raising the volume, using the diaphragm, expanding our ability to articulate, develops the muscle strength for a powerful voice. It might even change our minds about having one.

The remainder of Day Four focuses on communication and relationship. The next exercise indicates a position from which to start.

4C. Focus In/Eyes Out

• Stand face to face with a partner. Watch your breath. While you are looking directly at your partner, bring your attention, your focus, back inside your own body, as if you are looking out from the back of your own skull or spinal cord. A blurring or fading of vision might occur. Now, gradually bring your attention out until you're looking directly at your partner's face, and into their eyes. Project your energy out through your eyes into the eyes of your partner. More and more, and more, until you feel as if you're a laser beam, sending all the energy you can possibly blast out from your eyes into the eyes of your partner, through their eyes, and into their head. Now, bring your focus slowly back towards yourself. Move your focus back and forth between the back of your head or spinal cord, and their being, their eyes and yours, like a pendulum. Gradually let your focus settle in the middle:

right between your partner's eyes and the back of your own skull. Stay there. Become familiar with that sensation.

◟ •

Some people's attention is so fixed on their own experience that they're blind to what's going on around them. Others attach their attention onto what's going on around them so much, that they lose connection to their own experience. Most of us tip the scale more one way than the other, depending on the day, our mood, or what happens to hook our interest. If we're not careful, we can walk into a table, get hit by a train, forget to tuck in our shirt, or be blind to how we feel ourselves. In **Focus In/Eyes Out**, students play with shifting from inner to outer attention and back again. They may even discover their ability to hold it all simultaneously.

One of these states may feel more familiar. In a moment of conversation with their partner, students can identify which is their habitual tendency.

◟ •

4D. Mirroring

• Again, standing face to face, look directly in each other's eyes. Balance your attention evenly between you—some on your partner, some on yourself. Begin a mirroring exercise with a leader and a follower. One of you will become the leader by being the first to initiate movement.

• Leader, using movement and facial expression, project internal material—feelings, attitudes, and states of mind—onto your partner. Make your partner into different people who provoke you. Allow yourself to respond to your projection, to get totally involved, in who or what you've made your partner into.

• When you move, leader, move slow enough to allow your follower to mirror you exactly, synchronously; an outsider wouldn't be able to see who was leader and who was follower. So you have a projection going and your follower is totally falling into it—but doing you movements, not the ones your projection might have dictated.

• Follower, you don't know anything about what the leader is working with, but you do know what she does. You are the mirror image of the person in front of you. Allow the leader to enter your mind and body. Notice the detail of her body, the expression on her face, how your leader holds her face, its shape and tension. Take on her spirit. Experience what your leader seems to be experiencing and mirror that back.

• The two of you stay in eye-to-eye contact. If the leader looks away, the follower must look away, and lose the ability to follow exactly.

• When I say "Switch," without stopping, and continuing from right where you are, switch roles. I'm going to say switch several times, so you'll switch roles a couple times each.

• Now, I'm not going to say, "Switch." You decide when to take the leadership away from each other. Do this by *shifting*—stopping what you're doing and doing something else that is completely different from what you and your partner were just doing. At this time, don't worry about eye contact. Let your eyes focus appropriately onto whatever it is you are experiencing. Move at any speed and travel through the room if necessary. Have the *shifts*, the interruptions,

Mirroring

or lead-taking, come faster and faster. Follower, do the best you can to keep up.

• Add the voice and make all action into sound and movement action.

• Add language. Each time either of you *shifts,* and assumes the role of leader, begin a monologue very different from the one you interrupted. Keep up with one another as best you can. Simplify your movement. Have your physical action be appropriate to your language. If necessary, don't move at all, and, by all means, if your talking, don't walk. Find another physical form to accompany your language.

Leading and following affect people's emotions. Can we enter the mirroring game and set aside our judgments about the actions we carry out? Can we separate our predetermined emotions from the actual experience of action?

Following has a reputation for being passive, demeaning, or lacking creativity and initiative. Therefore, some people are more comfortable leading. Others are more comfortable following. Leading has connotations of being aggressive, demanding and egotistical. If we're focused on the moment-to-moment transaction between ourselves and our partners, it doesn't really matter which activity we do. What matters is that we can sense when we should follow someone or take leadership away. We become comfortable with switching off from leader to follower, depending on the task to be accomplished, while not being attached to either position.

The task is to truly lead when leading, without self-consciousness inhibiting your actions, and to truly follow when following, graciously and generously.

Information (thoughts, images, memories, physical sensations, sounds, etc.) comes into our awareness. We identify or interpret this information. We name it. We make judgments about what we have named based on our historical relationship to the material. Emotions arise as reactions to these judgments. Most of the time, we're not aware of this process.

We believe our emotions are as real as the thoughts and opinions that inspired them. We say, "This is how I really feel," or "This is how I really think," or even "This is who I really am." And, in fact, as long as we believe that such and such is real, it is. What we don't *real-ize* is that outside of the raw experience that came into our awareness, everything has been made up. For example:

> *A woman hears a sound in the distance. She identifies the sound and calls it, "Train." She judges the train to be dangerous because of a childhood event, in which she witnessed a rail accident. As a result, she is overwhelmed with anxiety every time she hears a train.*

Alternatively, this woman could hear a sound and not identify it. Simply listen to the sound—a long drawn out whistle or three sharp blasts of air—whatever. If she stays in the experience of listening without any interpretation, she could work with the sound as she desires. She could allow the sound to lead her toward a fresh perception, rather than having her own interpretation repeatedly limit her experience.

If we stick to exactly what comes into our awareness, and not embellish it with meaning, we're more likely to experience a fresh perception of constantly changing events.

In this theater training, students become familiar with the process of manufacturing reality. Over and over, they live out situations that they makeup on the spot. They makeup beliefs, emotions and feelings that are as "real" as day-to-day ones.

By making-up experience, whether it be beliefs, emotions, feelings or images, students recognize that they are not that material. The fictions are simply configurations of mind/body energies passing through the performer, accompanied by personal history or devoid of it. This necessary distance helps us to experience any and all realities.

The **Mirroring** exercise invited experience without interpretation. Partners simultaneously perceived, accepted and responded no matter whether they were leader or follower. If the leader's attention is wholly upon the follower and vice-a-versa, then their consciousnesses merge—

both are lost to the giving and receiving. Leaders are watching the followers so much they're picking up clues to follow. Followers mirror with such attention and tenacity, that they begin to lead themselves into experience.

Automatic Pilot

Why are students asked not to walk and talk at the same time? Because we usually walk and talk simultaneously and unconsciously. Our attention is on the content of the talking and we leave our legs to fend for themselves. We trust that they will figure out right, left, right, left, in the proper order toward the desired destination. To get out of this "automatic pilot" state, we can become aware of all our activities. We play with the physical relationship between walking and talking, knowing that their relationship makes meaning. For example:

> John is pacing back and forth along the edge of the carpet. He is describing the demise of a relationship. His pacing and his language consciously intersperse. His tone is reflected in the jerky, angry energy of his walk. When his voice pauses, you can hear his narration continue in his walk. As he reaches different emotional states in his story, we see change in each stride and word, the dropping or lifting of energy, direction, expressions on his face, breathing. Sadness, anger, despair, rage at not being understood make his timing irregular. He speaks through his movement as well as his speech. There's tension between the words and the steps. His audience experiences the full onslaught of both actions combined.

4E. Accumulation, One Leader

• Form trios with two new partners. You are going to build compositions, or small scenes using the *shift* technique. One of you will be the provider. You will introduce all the material for the scene. The other two may only mirror what you do, exactly as you have done it, but not necessarily when you do it. You'll do this exercise three times so that each of you will have a turn being the provider.

• Begin by standing in a neutral posture, legs shoulder width apart, spine straight, eyes forward, arms hanging at your sides.

• Provider: Using movement, sound and movement, or language and movement, introduce three to five very different modes of behavior. By "mode," I mean a state of being expressed by an accompanying action. Not simply repeatable movements, but ways of behaving—constellations of physical, vocal and/or verbal behavior that have feeling and meaning.

• For example, you may move in a particular quality, bent over, hands grabbing at head, expressing confusion, or sound and move in a particular way expressing animal-like greed, or shout, "Where is the child?" while striding frantically across the room.

• Make them clear so that your partners have no trouble deciphering your intention; get meaning behind the act. Make sure that everybody in your group can see and hear the mode when you do it. You may have to repeat it a few times.

• Each of the modes you introduce should be very different from the others. Different in content and form, movement quality, timing, the space it uses, and the tension, or energy, it carries.

• After the provider introduces one mode, all three of you interact using only this first mode, until the provider introduces a second. Then, the three of you have two modes to interact with. Eventually, you may end up with as many as five modes.

• Remember you're interacting, not just copying. You are building a scene out of just a few elements. The provider is not the leader. Independently you decide when to do each mode. The three of you are collaborating in the development of a relationship; watching, listening and responding to each other, you use the modes provided as your language.

• Provider, stay connected to what is going on inside of you and focus on your partners. Each mode you introduce is a response to your inner and outer awareness—what you notice in yourself and what you notice about what they're doing. You'll provide all of the actions, but the event develops as a collaboration.

• All of you: consider how you're using the space, pauses, and stillness. You can't all be active all the time, or you won't be able to watch each other, read cues and respond. Pause within your action, but don't ever return to neutral once the improvisation has begun.

• Continue until I say, "One minute," then find a place to stop.

Bulking

Even though participants copy the material laid down by the initiator, they need not feel invisible. By joining an action, and adding their body to it, they're **bulking** the image. Bulking strengthens and draws focus to an action. Bulking makes replicas of actions and uses them to enhance the improvisation, bringing weight and importance.

If a person initiates a shift by standing still, talking about eagles with an airy, windy manner, and gesturing with their hands as they speak, then another person can bulk this image by doing exactly the same thing. They can stand behind them or in another corner, but they must not change the form.

Neutral

We make covenants in this training—terms and signals that we agree upon. "Neutral" is one of these. It refers to a posture that is as empty of meaning as possible: standing erect, arms relaxed at sides, weight balanced between both feet, eyes front, relaxed face. No posture can ever really be neutral. But, we've assigned that meaning to this one, a meaning of "Empty. Ready to begin."

Contrast

A frog sits on a leaf by the edge of a pond. Everything around her is still. Suddenly, she perceives movement, a black dot enters her field of vision. Snap! Lunch!

Frogs can only see contrast. They see edges, movement, and dimming or brightening. With just these few observations, they find food, shelter, water, mates and live their life.

Frogs, like people, gather information about their environment by perceiving contrast between elements in relationship. People notice one thing, only because they notice another: movement in relation to stillness, sound in relation to silence, loud in relation to soft, fast to slow, heavy to light, black/white, tension/relaxation, and on and on.

Without contrast, there's no new information. For instance, if you want to go to sleep, you limit your information, you count sheep. The same sheep, over and over again, jumping the same fence. The weather doesn't change. Nobody comes along. A sheep doesn't trip on the fence. Monotony moves in. Good night.

If you want to put the people at your dinner table to sleep, or your audience, then don't change anything. Not the movements, pacing, or dynamics. No surprises. No jolts. Keep everything on an even keel. They'll be nodding off in no time.

To keep an improvisation alive, one of the necessary elements is contrast. Things have to differ from one another. It's the edges, movements, and dimmings, or brightenings, that keep us interested. If we see contrast in an improvisation, then we're more likely to be interested. If we don't, we usually end up looking for it anyway.

All the actions don't have to be different; contrast can be found in any of the elements that compose an action. A trio may be doing only one action for a long time and still keep us interested if the timing of that action has contrast, or their placement in the room, their movement, sound volume, rhythm, breath, eyes offers some contrast.

Accumulation, One Leader offers the student an opportunity to experiment with contrasting actions.

Any feeling or state of mind can be expressed in an infinite number of ways. Look at anger, for example.

To express anger, you could:

1. Clench fists, hold breath and curse under it, turn red in the face, pace back and forth.

   or

2. Bang fist on table, dart eyes quickly around the room, tighten lips, breathe fast.

   or

3. Throw objects against the wall, scream accusations at another person in the room, occasionally throw an object at other person.

   or

4. Sit in a relaxed posture at the table, breathe normally, rhythmically gouge a mark deeper and deeper into the table with a pencil.

   or

5. Smile all the time.

   or

6. Sway back and forth while tugging at your clothing, taking very deep inhalations and exhalations, softly moaning on every 4th and 9th breath.

   or

7. Sporadically turn in a circle, while saying names of men and women in a loud voice.

   or

8. Wipe a window with a feather while flaring your nostrils. And on and on . . .

All of these and just about anything else will work if the action carries the intention of anger. Meaning comes from a combination of what you do and how you do it.

We emphasize **form** in order to expand awareness and awaken a greater range of expression. To prevent students from over-focusing on form, losing touch and becoming mechanical, they're reminded to clarify their intention. Clear form requires clear intention. Stay with feeling.

4F. Performance Score: Accumulation, All Leading

• Three people go out on the floor. The rest of us are your audience. We're going to repeat the accumulation exercise. However, we'll change the structure a bit. Rather than having one person be the provider as before, each of you will provide at least one mode of behavior, but no more than two.

• Be aware of the audience and orient yourselves to include them. Keep your composition open so the audience can share your experience.

Our relationship to the audience and our partners changes depending upon where our attention is. If our attention is inward, then our partners, or audience, become voyeurs who observe our imaginings from the outside. If our attention is outward, we can either engage or not engage our partners, or audience, depending on how we focus that attention. When we single out a partner or an audience member, look at them directly in the eyes, we set up intimacy that demands response; when we look in their direction but not directly at them, no response is demanded, even though we may be sharing ourselves intimately with them.

How a performer directs her attention defines the wall between herself and the audience. The wall may have densities, from transparent to opaque. This depends upon the nature of the situation and what the performer senses will best serve it.

Composition

An improvisation is a series of actions. Composition refers to the make-up of these action, their relationship to one another, their order and design. A composition is organized information. For that information to be clear, one act must be perceived distinctly from another. Contrast allows distinction.

Some improvisations are cohesive. Something holds all the pieces together. Some aren't, and are arbitrary strings of events.

Walking Backwards and Laying Down Stones

Improvising is like walking backwards. You can see where you've been, but you can't see where you're going. But what you see does affect where you're going.

As you improvise, you lay down stones of action. In a sense, you create a path. You hold all of the stones in your awareness and that awareness effects your current action. As long as you stay aware and remember the stones you've laid down, your current action can't help but be responsive and relevant to your previous actions. The whole thing will be cohesive.

In a cohesive composition, inner and outer awareness work hand-in-hand. They release new material, and simultaneously examine the path that has been travelled. The stones may make sense laying in order, one after another, or they might make sense uprooted and replanted in a new spot. As you put down new stones and reuse old ones, the piece begins to take its own shape. Patterns may appear that ask for further development. You don't have to wonder what it's about. It tells you itself. Simply pay attention to what has occurred and keep responding.

Imagine that you are rowing a boat down the center of a narrow bay. Usually, when you row a boat you face away from where you're going. From this orientation, it looks like you travel back-

wards. You see where you've been, yet, you don't see where you're going. By watching the shoreline, gauging the distance between your craft and the right and left banks, you can steady your course, and maneuver right down the center.

On Day Four students balance inner and outer awareness. They practice fiercely holding onto and easily giving up one reality after another. It didn't matter whether that reality was generated by themselves or by their partner. They explored the merits of contrast and how it affects clear communication and composition. They played with the understanding that by completely investing in their fictional experiences, their experiences become real.

Inner/Outer

5A. Eyes Closed
5B. Jog Patterns
5C. Only Verbs
5D. Say What You Do
5E. Performance Score: Say What You Do Together
5F. Performance Score: Bench: Head/Arm/Leg

Take a walk. Ride into the country. Go to the beach. Be with nature as much as possible this month—a potted plant, a candle, a bowl of water. In order to remember, it's necessary to clear away the debris.

Inner

Students practice experiencing and expressing feelings, all kinds of feelings, even feelings that possibly surround painful "real-life" experiences.

They often fear that during exercises "real-life" material that is shameful or hurtful will surface. They fear they'll lose control, get lost in themselves and never recover.

Suppose, for example, the first time someone speaks in public they lose their train of thought. They sit down, embarrassed and disoriented. They feel shame and attach this shame to the action of public speaking. Thereafter, every time they feel the urge to speak in public, they project shame onto that action, create an unpleasant experience and quell their desire. This condition remains permanent until they consciously examine it.

Years later, in a training such as this, they begin to examine shame and the physical expressions of it. Again, they feel shame spontaneously arising. But this time, shame surfaces within a different context. As they experience shame, they notice a configuration of elements (breath, temperature, tension, quality of motion, voice, etc.) that comprises shame. It's no longer stigmatic "shame." It's just a feeling and sensation that can be noticed. The relationship to public speaking alters. Previously constructed shame no longer stifles action.

5A. Eyes Closed

• Find a place for yourself on the floor, either sitting, standing or lying down. Get comfortable and close your eyes. Bring your attention inside. Relax. Watch your breath: your inhalation, exhalation, the pause in between. As your breath goes out, let go of any tension you're aware of either in your mind or body, or both. Become still and quiet, so that your attention may settle entirely on the experience of your breath.

• Keep your eyes closed for the next fifteen to twenty minutes.

• You can begin moving at any time. Start with any impulse. Do exactly what you feel like doing. A twitch, stretch, bend, contraction, an expansion, or jerk. Allow that movement to cue the next. Continue to follow them, one movement cueing the next movement, that movement cueing the next.

• Whatever feelings, emotions, attitudes or states of mind arise, play with them, express them through your movement, the tension in your body and the expression on your face. Continue to follow your physical sensations . . .

• Whatever you're doing right now, intensify . . .

• Whatever you're doing right now, intensify . . .

• Accept invitations as your body presents them: If you're moving with soft-ness, be really soft. If you're moving into a hard, tense place, go further into that. If you're moving into a painful place, go further into it. If you're moving into fun and play, go further. If you're moving into any unidentified state right now, go further into it. Whatever you're doing right now, intensify . . .

• Work up a sweat if that's what's up. Breathe hard if that's what's up. If you come in contact with another person in the room, do whatever it is you want. Play with it. Mess with it. Get tense. Get loose. Do whatever it is you want. If you want to leave and travel on your journey alone, leave. Whatever you're doing right now, intensify . . .

• Take this twenty minute period to move through an inner journey of mind and body, whatever that may be. Don't try to understand it and don't try to create it. Give your body the time to speak.

• Be still right where you are . . . Now, open your eyes, maintaining a relaxed focus, your eyelids half-open. Let your gaze rest about ten feet in front of you. As your attention returns to the room, open your eyes more but keep your focus soft. Come to standing and begin a very slow walk . . . As you walk bring your attention back into this room, allow the others to come into your awareness.

Protection

We have learned to separate from our experience, to relate to it as an object to be analyzed, evaluated and planned. But, somewhere inside us, another type of experiencing calls. For some, it calls loudly and insists on a response.

In **Eyes Closed,** students have the opportunity to give up all the chatter, quiet the mind and follow experience without comment. This is often terrifying. It's so unfamiliar. Vulnerable. Unprotected. It's frightening to enter a state, or condition, that is unfamiliar and can't be called anything. Fear of the unknown, of getting into what we don't want to, of going into an "other" state and not coming back, fear of being crazy, all prevent us from examining those states.

By entering the states we fear again and again, taking small doses a little at a time, we build up tolerance for those states. Our capacity increases. In action, repeated entrances, fear lessens. We enter the nameless states which are bound by fear as investigators and become aware of what is inside. The actions are viewed as what they are, instead of the mythology we have given them.

We step into the unknown with awareness. We build survival skills with this awareness. Eventually, judgment vanishes and only inquisitiveness remains. We don't need protection when there's no fear. Awareness itself is the protection.

An exercise such as **Eyes Closed** offers inroads into the mysterious territories of mind. Students new to this experience often approach it hesitantly. They need to feel their way. They need to know where they are. They may move with their arms outstretched, fingers reaching, feeling the floor, walls and others as if they are blind. In fact, they are. They're blind to their habitual responses in a visual world. They're still attached to this external visual world, and resist going inside themselves for information. As they practice and gain confidence step by step, their fear begins to leave.

In the darkness, one slips inward. With eyes closed, there are less distractions—nothing to see, no lights, colors, shapes. No people. Even the student isn't there, in a sense, the familiar sense.

We repeat this exercise several times in the training, each time offering a further excursion into the unfamiliar.

Privacy

Privacy is a myth. We support it with two beliefs. The first is that we "have" a limited amount of "material" (secrets), and that if we reveal them, we'll be out of the material, left empty. The second belief is that our inner world and our outer world are different, and that privacy is the watchdog that keeps them separate.

All phenomena, whether secrets, chocolate, or trees, are either totally you, or totally not you. They're all constructions of the mind. Personal stories, the ones kept under wraps, are burdens better to be lifted into the lightness of expression. Every secret kept is a blockade, a stone stuck in the mouth of a cave of memories, images, convictions, emotions and surprises. What we keep hidden, we are hiding from.

> *Three students are out on the floor improvising: inching along together, dripping and leaking bits and pieces of their psyche, lightening up, upping the ante of what's worth putting effort into, what's worth expressing, what's drawing their attention. The rest of us are audiencing. Through the course of their ten minute improvisation, they experience and express many states of mind: emotions (envy, anger, lust, complacency, etc.), attitudes (pride, passivity, secretiveness, etc.) and un-nameable, yet recognizable, conditions.*

Audiencing

When they're finished, we talk about it. The audience tells them what aspects of their event they "connected" to and what aspects they didn't. By "connected," we mean that we recognized, or identified with, the performer's experience; their bodies communicated directly. No thought, analysis or interpretation.

We identify with a state of mind because we have experienced that same condition in our own lives. But there are states we haven't directly experienced, yet we feel they reside in our psyche. We may not be able to identify them but they are recognizable, states stored in all human experience. Maybe you've witnessed someone in a trance state exhibiting exotic behavior, or an autistic child rocking back and forth, their mind obviously elsewhere, or the Whirling Dervishes. These may not be experiences you have had, but if you relax and fully accept them through your body in the moment, you will find them familiar.

If the audience doesn't connect to the experience of the performer, it's because of one of two reasons. Either, the performer has distanced herself from what she is expressing and is not reflecting her immediate experience—audiences are uncomfortable with the discrepancy between the performer and the performance, the space within which the performer is judging, planning, dying. They feel that something's not right. They're being bamboozled—or, the audience, for whatever reason, is not letting the actor's intention touch them.

Being audience to one another is part of our education. It's another way to stretch and experience ourselves. We watch each other drip and leak, then we speak from our individual recognitions. When we perform, we repeatedly dispel secrets from our private worlds; when we are in the audience watching others, we recognize those secrets. Our voices talk of humanness. Nothing's personal.

"Privacy" is a burdensome concept.

5B. Jog Patterns

• Walk. Accelerate. Walk even faster. Keep changing your direction. Avoid circling the room. Change your direction spontaneously, don't think about it. Accelerate. Accelerate more. Accelerate until you're jogging. An easy jog. As you're jogging, bring everyone else into your awareness. Where are they? Where are you in relation to them?

• Begin to build patterns, spatial designs or games together. You all see the same pattern developing and you all contribute and collaborate on its execution. You are only playing with space, jogging, either in place, or travelling. Nothing else. There is only one spatial pattern in the room at any one time and everyone is involved in it. No duets. Keep your eye on the group.

• Patterns are going to change: one person, introduce a new spatial element. The group, either incorporate that new element into the existing pattern, or begin a new pattern with it.

Jog patterns focuses on action. It's athletic and easy. There's no story or language. It's about ensemble. It's about herding—moving as a pack in the same time and space and with the same intention. Events happen too fast for anything else.

Patterns require agreement. The mind must let go of itself to accommodate and alter the group energy and design. Everyone must follow by leading and lead by following. What if everyone threw their orange peels on the highway? In **Jog Patterns**, private agendas don't work:

* I have a great idea. I'll do it this way.
* Pheww!! I'll get lost in the crowd.

If everyone had great ideas and executed them there could be a splendiferous show of chaos but there'd be no patterns. And, if everyone hid in the crowd, one pattern would repeat itself ad infinitum.

The move from **Eyes Closed** directly to **Jog Patterns** is a radical change from inner to outer focus. Students respond to this in various ways. Some are particularly attached to their inner world and want to stay there. They resist being yanked away from home. Others feel imprisoned inside of themselves and can't wait to escape. Their home is social.

In **Eyes Closed**, the student follows and responds to the ever-changing landscape of her mind. In **Jog Patterns**, the student follows and responds to the ever-changing landscape of the group activity. Similarities exist. As students practice shifting focus from inner to outer, and outer to inner, they experience awareness, no matter what the object of awareness may be. The content, whether it comes from an inner or outer orientation, turns less and less precious, less and less separate. It's all material of equal value.

5C. Only Verbs

• With partners. If possible, work with someone you haven't worked with before. One of you is speaker, and the other is mover.

• Speaker, you say only action verbs, such as walk, sit, stand, smile, clap, bend, etc. And as you say each verb, the mover will perform that action. If you say, "Sit," the mover will sit. If you say, "Stand," she will stand. If you say, "Lie down," she will lie down.

• Speaker, play with the way you say the verbs. Let your body/mind speak the verbs. Approach the saying of these verbs as a dance of changeability, a reflection of your shifty interior. Go for range. Allow for vast variety in the way you say the verbs. Change your mind, irrationally, radically. Even inside of one verb, change your mind several times. Your language responds to feeling. Feeling is in the body. The body is dynamic.

• Mover, you will reflect the speaker's quality of speech with how you perform the action. Every nuance in the speaker's voice, every chatter of teeth, push of breath, every pause, shows up in your movement. You are the physical embodiment of the speaker's sound. Because the speaker plays with the sounds of the words, you might not be able to hear what the verb is, what action you are supposed to be doing. That's fine. Go with the sounds/energies you hear/feel at the time. You move only when you hear sound. However long it takes the speaker to complete the word, you take the same amount of time to complete your action. It may be two minutes before the speaker reaches "k" in the word "walk." In that time period, you are to carry the same dynamic as the speaker's voice. Don't look at the speaker. Create your own world.

• Speaker, your primary function through the speaking of these verbs is to explore your interior world, not to order the mover around. You may watch the mover, however, and allow her spirit and action to influence your interior path.

◝ •

Dancing the Mouth

Speech is movement. Like any movement, speech has the potential for strength, agility, and grace. All these parts move: tongue, teeth, upper jaw, lower jaw, gums, hard palate, soft palate, cheeks and lips. We sense this movement, moment by moment. The interaction of these moving parts, combined with breath and voice, articulates vocal sound. We hear that sound moment to moment. The movement and the sound combined affect our psyche and change our reality. We respond to that change with the next movement, the next feeling, the next sound. We're tuning into the loop of action/awareness/action.

the instrument
sparks the psyche
the psyche
sparks the instrument

Just as **Eyes Closed** has the potential to focus attention on one aspect of the self, so does the voice. The mind must quiet down so that attention can rest on each moment of sound, so that one can discover the sensuality that waits.

> *Take the word "sit." There are infinite possibilities. Worlds. Say, "Sit." Now, say, "Sit," as if you mean: Hello; or, I love you; or, Get out of here; or, Come back; or, I'm fed up; or, Stop that; or, I'm dizzy, I'm terrified, I'm dissolving; or, I'm speechless, confused, constricted, choking.*

As in the **Mirroring** exercise, **Only Verbs** offers students opportunity to look at belief relative to function and role. Here, the functions are simply to speak verbs, or respond with movement. Carrying out these functions may produce uncomfortable feelings associated with the roles of "being in command" and "being commanded." Feelings accompanying certain actions may lead to positions of power and oppression, and to roles of victor and victim. Through this exercise, students may see that such feelings are reflexive conditions, not necessarily relevant to their current experience, but generated from past occasions.

Once freed from habitual feelings about the roles being played, students can hear language as cues for choreography and maps for inner exploration. The mover and the speaker will then have infinite choice.

They focus on their immediate experience and expression and bypass role identification.

5D. Say What You Do

• Leave your partners. You'll be working alone, putting the two functions of the previous exercise together. You will be both speaker and mover, simultaneously. Say a verb, preceded by the word "I," and perform the action that the word signifies. As you say, "I sit," you sit. As you say, "I stand," you stand, etc. You are not speaking without movement and not moving without speech. The way the word is spoken and the way the action is executed happen at the same moment, with the same energy, feeling, and meaning. Experiment with changing your mind, which will change your expression, once or even several times, within the enunciation of a single verb.

• You may pause between expressions, or inside each expression. When you're still, you will be silent. When you're silent, you will be still.

This has moved sound and movement into language. Saying, "I sit," and simultaneously sitting is a single action that emanates from the whole body as a single source. Neither speech, nor action lead. Finding this source takes some investigation, some practice. Students practice this until they feel secure in the technique, until there's no arbitrary movement, and until the speech and the motion are bound exactly, and surrounded by silence and stillness. Once this happens, they are ready to explore this form in relationship.

5E. Performance Score:
Say What You Do, Together

• One pair out on the floor, the rest of us will be audience.

• Both of you will now bring what you were just practicing into relationship. By saying what you are doing while you are doing it ("I" plus simple active verbs), you'll be in *continuous response* to each other. You're in a dialogue, alternating turns, maybe sometimes overlapping. You're watching and listening, in detail, constantly observing the cues that each other offers. Suppose your partner says, "I look," and looks away from you with abrupt alertness. You may respond with, "I look," and also look where they're looking, or anything else that comes to mind in response. You don't have to think anything up. Your partner is providing all the information that you need. Just believe them. In effect, they're telling you what to do. You only have to respond.

• Listen to your partner's voice. Listen to your voices together. Hear the rhythmic and tonal patterns. Respond to your partner's shapes, changes, feelings. There's no missed beats between you.

⌣ •

Adding relationship to the detail-oriented technique of the **Only Verbs** exercise challenges students to remain conscious of their experience as they receive and respond to their partner's experience. All of this in front of an audience. There's a lot going on that's demanding attention.

The last exercise of the day is simple, a relief from the gathering demands.

⌣ •

5F. Performance Score: Bench: Head, Arm, Leg

• I've put a bench out on the floor. Three people sit on the bench and face the audience. You can only do three actions: raise an arm, turn your head, or cross a leg. That's all. Interact with these three actions.

Detail

Language is eliminated. Students are left with hardly anything at all. So it seems. Only three simple and common actions with which to build a

Head, Arm, Leg

world full of thoughts, feelings, desires, actions and responses. A world that's about three people sitting on a bench.

The details do it. The slightest movement describes an entire story. A head turns with a particular musicality and tension. An eyebrow lifts. An expression on a face changes and changes again, and we know the inner story.

Students discover how little is needed. When action is stripped down, subtleties capture the focus. The slight turn of a hand may indicate a catastrophe.

Day Five leads students on a back-and-forth voyage. They travel from the inner mind, the personal, to the outer ensemble, the contextual, and from the inner world of language to the outer world of relationship. They discover that details provide directive arrows as guides from internal awareness toward expressive composition. Back-and-forth, a see-saw of attention. They strive for a restful place, a fulcrum, a balanced center between all of their worlds.

They're picking, poking and looking at themselves. If what they're doing isn't enrapturing, nothing is gained. Analysis doesn't create change. It only adds information to the already existing over-abundance. Changes occur through awareness. Even though students stumble and bumble, analyze and try, they eventually, sooner or later, give up and start to play. Then all the trying, the practice, the intelligence and information-gathering, is laid aside. But it doesn't go away. It joins the cache of wisdom that directs their lives.

Pretend to Pretend

6A. Hard Lines/Soft Curves
6B. "Ahs" and "Ooohs"
6C. Empty Vessel
6D. Solo Shifts
6E. Performance Score: Back to Front, Silent

The performer's timing is a dead give away as to whether they're "pretending" or "pretending to pretend." If they're pretending, they're separated from their actions. Their mind is somewhere else, watching, judging, planning. Their actions aren't spontaneous. They miss beats because their thoughts create a space between perception and response. The audience senses this lapse, this deadness. It's evident that the performer has latched onto his/her own uncertainties and, at least, at that moment, is not in the flow.

Pretending to pretend, presupposes that all behavior is an "act." Performers are simultaneously, "in" and "on top" of every act, committed to every moment of change. Their responses are fast. They flow.

Day Six, as every other day in the training, begins with the body. As students become more deeply immersed in content, the danger of leaving the body lurks. An examined body offers untold information from which content can be drawn.

My body has a shape, a life, of its own. Where does its softness come from and its jitteriness? My hands have learned to clench their fists and my shoulders tighten. My legs spread when I sleep and my feet curl? My body knows that posture. My head tilts to the side when I run and I wave my arms in the space above, cutting sharp angles as if I'm whipping up a fire. My body is odd and ancient, while my young eyes grab in wonder. Awkward gestures speak of magic, and a simple step graces itself with a millennium of practice. My body can be big with the might of darkness or light, and yet, I am shy.

Unexpected magic that surprises doesn't come in one package. It isn't tinsel wrapped. It can look like anything. When you reach into that box of magic, you don't know what you're going to get.

All of the exercises in this training lead the student to magic. Only she can reach into it.

6A. Hard Lines/Soft Curves

• Find yourself a place on the floor and stand still. Watch your breath. With each exhalation, release any tension that you are aware of. On the inhalation, continue to send that tension out and away from your body. With each breath, become more quiet and more still.

• I'm going to call out words that indicate particular qualities of movement. Improvise movement within these qualities. By improvise, I mean that you make it up as you go along. When you hear each consecutive word, shift abruptly into the prescribed quality.

Hard lines
Soft curves
Vibrations
Jumps
Heavy lines

Angular paths
Complicated circles
Percussive starts and stops
Jumps and turns
Thrusts and stabs
Swings
Spirals

• As your body moves through these different physical modes, states of mind—emotions, feelings, and attitudes—may come into your awareness. Manifest these states through your actions—tension in your body, expression on your face, focus of your eyes.

• Within the next few minutes, associate with someone else in the room and interact with them using these same qualities. I'm not going to call them out. You're body knows them by now. You decide when to change from one to another. The choice will depend on what your partner is up to. Be clear. Keep the qualities distinct. You and your partner may interact with similar or contrasting qualities. These qualities are your language. Talk to each other.

Putting our bodies in unfamiliar shapes can be as awkward as trying to speak a foreign language. It takes time for the experience to become comfortable.

When we're studying a foreign language, we're happy just to use the right word at the right time. As we become more fluent, our lives become influenced by that language and how it orders and describes perception. Our experience becomes concretized by the collective intelligence of those who speak the same tongue.

In **Hard Lines/Soft Curves** students explore movement as language. Instead of rolling their "r's," they roll their hips. Instead of sharpening their consonants, they sharpen their thrusts and jabs, expanding and articulating their newly acquired movement vocabulary. At first, they approach it technically, as a task. At some point, students let go of movement as technique and they just move. The movement is guided by its own voice and moves itself.

Different qualities of movement inspire different moods. Different moods and aspects of mind call for different qualities of movement. Body and imagination work in tandem, pushing and pulling each other into new terrain.

Breath Again

Breath goes deep. When we turn our attention to it, we can feel it. It's one of the few things inside that we can feel. It's a channel leading to our inner body awareness.

Our inner body (organs, vessels, nerves, fluids, muscles) and our outer body (skin, facial features, fingers and toes, legs and arms) don't appear to have much to do with each other. In fact, for most of us, the outer body seems to run the whole show. If it moves, then we know the body is moving. If it's still, then we assume the body is still. We often forget that our skin covers up the biggest parade in town. Pumps, squeezes, charges, thrusts, leaps, oozes and every other possible movement follow one another in a never ending procession. Within a single cell, there's enough squeezing and jostling, consuming, discharging, entering and exiting to make the outer body seem asleep in comparison.

Yet, out of all that commotion, we can find our breath. Through our breath, we find our voice.

6B. "Ahs" and "Ooohs"

• Everybody walk. Watch your breath. The air comes in, bounces out, then there's a pause. The next time you exhale, drop your mouth, and exhale with a whispered "ah" sound. Not a sigh but a steady stream of air. Inhale, then exhale with a whispered "ah." Hang your mouth open. Open mouth, open "ah" sound. Add voice and with each breath, increase the volume of the "ah." Use your diaphragm. Stay relaxed. Throat, shoulders and face, relaxed. The air comes in, bounces out, small voice, "ah," and then there's a pause. Two steps for your inhale, two steps for your exhale with the "ah." Two steps inhale, two steps exhale with "ah." Change the "ah" to "oooh." Two steps, inhale, two steps, "oooh . . . oooh." Now, four "ooohs" on two steps, inhale, two steps, on the exhale, "oooh . . . oooh . . . oooh . . . oooh." Combine the two sounds. Two steps, inhale, two steps exhale with "ah . . . ah . . . oooh . . . oooh . . . oooh . . . oooh."

Danger: Watching the breath may have a down-side. You might use your breath to escape from an uncomfortable current experience, to retreat. Fade away.

Example: Suppose you're agitated. What are you supposed to do? Breathe. When overwhelmed? What are you supposed to do? Breathe. Upset in any way? Breathe. But have the feelings gone away? No, they're still there, waiting in the wings.

Instead: An alternative is to look at agitation. What's it all about? And upsetting and overwhelming feelings? Examine them directly. Go into them. Feel them. Work with them. Work through them. Take the time it takes to explore them without being subsumed or submerged by them, with a space of detachment. "This is what I feel like when I am very angry." Or very scared. Or very anxious.

We're not always lucky enough to have feelings surface to be explored or played with. Sometimes, we just make them up.

Useful Faking

If we practice a behavior long enough, that behavior may become second nature. We must be careful of what we practice.

"That felt fake." "I was faking it." Well, then fake it. Really fake it. The fake space is the space between the doer and what's being done. In these instances, the performer is distracted and withholds feeling from their action. Withholding, then, is what takes place in the space between performer and action. So, really withhold. What does withholding feel like?

How does it move? Speak? What does it have to say?

After an exercise, when a student comes back with, "That felt fake," or "I faked it," a question that needs to be addressed is: What did that feel like? What were the physical sensations that comprised that experience? Instead of judging, it's time to investigate. The negative judgment aligned with "fake" causes discomfort. Withhold judgment and just let feelings be feelings, empty of content.

> *Terry was recounting a mountain climbing event. She was trying to impart the heightened state of excitement and often terror that accompanied the experience. But it just wasn't working. She was pushing on the words, speeding up her language, her eyes and general energy, too expanded. Suppose, instead, Terry had relaxed and told the story from a present perspective. She would let the telling of the story inform her emotional responses. She would find out what the event means to her right now. Her concern would be less on how we receive the story and more on her own experience of telling it.*
>
> *But, suppose Terry is in a play and must recount the story with a heightened energy intended to recapture the excitement and terror of the event, night after night. She must focus on her physical as well as contextual experience, the interactive dance between her body, feelings, voice and text. She must become the expressive body itself rather then "maker" of the story.*

The following exercise brings students back to shifts with, again and again, the practice of immediately and fully accepting experience.

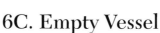

6C. Empty Vessel

• In quartets, one person steps out and faces the remaining three. That person is called the Empty Vessel. They begin by standing in a neutral position. The three partners, which we call Messengers, *one at a time*, bombard the Empty Vessel with different ways, or conditions, of being. As soon as one of the Messengers approaches and presents the empty vessel with a way of being, the Empty Vessel immediately copies the form and intention. Once the Empty Vessel has copied the form and intention of the Messenger, the two of them collaborate on an interaction within that mode of behavior. They don't change that mode, expand it, shrink it, or do anything else to it. They continue to interact until another Messenger interrupts. This Messenger captures the attention of the Empty Vessel and presents the Empty Vessel with a very different condition of being. The next Messenger enters

and replaces the first Messenger, who fades out. The process repeats. The Empty Vessel copies the form and intention of the next Messenger and the two interact.

• The Messengers enter at random and fairly quickly. There is no turn-taking. Whoever has an impulse approaches the Empty Vessel, driving out the former Messenger.

• The Messenger approaches the Empty Vessel expressing her currently imagined condition using one of the following forms: movement only, movement with vocalization, vocalization only, speech and movement, or only speech. She is completely engaged, mind and body. The spirit and actions are cohesive.

• Messengers, your job is to expand the range of the Empty

Vessel. Not just her physical range, but her psychological and expressive range. To do that, you yourselves have to travel into outer boundaries.

• Messengers, from where do you get your inspiration? Experience the interaction of the Empty Vessel and the Messenger right before you. What's your response to that experience? Your response is what you interrupt and move in with.

• After each set, the group stops for a chat. The Empty Vessel tells the Messengers if s/he experienced any patterns going on. In other words, did Messenger One always come in with violent behaviors? Did Messenger Two come in to calm things down? Did Messenger Three come in with material that had dancerly form with little or no intention or feeling? Was there an over-abundance of relationship quibbling, or mechanical movement, or language? What areas of the human psyche were left out? Was there clear contrast in the material presented? You can give yourselves tasks for the next round, so that everybody increases their expressive vocabulary.

• Rotate so that everyone in the quartet has a turn at being the Empty Vessel.

Empty Vessel simulates and stimulates spontaneity. Many students believe they cannot be spontaneous, but as "vessel," they travel through a flow of radical shifts of realities without forethought. They don't have to make it up. That's the job of the Messengers. With multiple messenger approaches, the Vessel quickly copies actions and gets an approximation of a spontaneous experience. Within this approximation, lie clues for self-directed spontaneous action.

Messengers stand on the outside knowing that they will soon approach the Vessel with a condition of being. What do they do while they're standing there? They observe and feel through their bodies the interaction between the Vessel and the current Messenger. They experience that interaction as if it were happening to them right then, right there. They

believe its reality, no distractions, no doubts. From their experiences responses spring. Not rationally, but irrationally, because the mind doesn't inhibit the body or the body inhibit the mind. An unsupressed imagination explodes.

The Messengers act as a unit, each responding to the one before, creating a scenario, cohesive chain of events, linked together by a collectively embodied imagination.

Parallel play: Two nine-month old humans are in a play pen. They each have a ball. They play with the balls independently, sometimes stopping to watch each other. It doesn't occur to them to share or interact. They are on their own course, in their own worlds.

Interaction: Two twenty-year old humans are in an empty room. They are each given a ball. They independently explore the balls. They will eventually throw and catch the balls to and from each other and even join in a common goal of trying to get the ball in a hoop.

As soon as the Vessel notices the entering Messenger, she joins the Messenger's world by doing what he is doing. The two don't play in this world side by side, unresponsive to each other. They play together, interacting, even though, they're doing the same thing. Their relationship is a dialogue. Of course, it's possible that the Messenger may introduce some form that calls for parallel play. Praying, or singing, for example. But, usually, a dialogue is appropriate.

Whether to join as a parallel or interactive partner is always a choice, no matter the form of the improvisation. Here, we're throwing light on behavior that we often perform automatically without awareness.

Does this sound familiar? You're in a locker room, changing clothes in preparation for a workout. Normally people parallel play this phenomena. No one looks at each other directly or addresses one another. Up until now, you've automatically behaved the same way. Today, you consciously see the structure of the situation. Now, you see you have a choice. You can abide by the conventions because you think they're reasonable or you can step through them by striking up a conversation with a person nearby. "I really like the new equipment, don't you?"

Subject/Subject and Subject/Object

If the Messenger (subject) says, "How are you?" and the Vessel (object) says, "Fine, thank you," a subject is talking to an object. If the Messenger says "How are you?" and the Vessel says, "How are you?" maintaining the intention of the Messenger, then the subject is being mirrored back to itself. Particularly with language, the Vessel and the Messenger interact not as subject/object but as subject/subject. They may subtly change the inflection to infuse the dialogue with tension and immediacy. They don't just parrot. They may even change the language as long as they maintain the Messenger's intention. For example, if the Messenger says "Get out of my office," the Vessel may say, "Get out of my store."

In our daily lives, people approach us all the time with agendas. We get caught up in their agendas and reinforce them. What the other demands, we assume we must respond to; we become objects to their subjects. We take on their reality as ours. They say, "You be my object." We say, "Oh, yes, okay."

> *A group of people are sitting in a circle together for the first time.*
> *They've been instructed to introduce themselves to one another.*
> *Someone starts. She says her name, how she feels about being*
> *with people she doesn't know, and what inspired her to come.*
> *One by one, the rest of the people proceed to follow her lead, say-*
> *ing, more or less, the same things—their names, how they feel*
> *about being there and why they came. No one thinks of breaking*
> *the mold the original person created. They just automatically fol-*
> *low. The ninth person does something different. After saying her*
> *name, she tells a little story about an event that happened to her*
> *that morning. Her story and its recounting gives insight into who*
> *she is.*

Suppose we find ourselves in disagreement with someone, not accepting their agenda, at loggerheads. If we maintain awareness and see the event from a detached perspective, these possibilities are open to us:

- We identify less with the outcome, thereby more easily adapting if the results are not in our favor.

- We experience the disagreement as an exercise of wits.

- We experience our seriousness with humor.

- We see our adversary as a partner in the creation of the argument's form and style.

- We see the form and style.

- We're not identified with winning anything, so we can let go of our position and listen.

- We feel comfortable letting opposing views co-exist and see interest in that.

- We're more open to sensing danger to our bodies or psyches.

In the **Empty Vessel** exercise, students consciously take on another's reality. Because they picked it up from their partner, they don't identify with it. It's not them. They experience this borrowed behavior as a combination of energy, feeling, form and belief. A costume to be experienced and released. Because it doesn't touch them personally, expose them in any way, they can get fully into it. There's nothing to lose.

Not identifying with someone else's reality is exactly what's required for students to consciously tune into their own inner experience while observant of another's passions. There's a difference between identifying and being. Suppose a Vessel is offered what appears to be an action of rage. They pick it up. If they identify with the rage, they may not be able to drop it when the next Messenger enters. There'll be a residue. Too much of their personal story gets hooked. If, on the other hand, they pick it up, knowing that this rage is not them, and don't even call it "rage," they can totally immerse themselves into the constellation of behavior that makes up this phenomenon. They become it. They need hold nothing back.

We can say that they pretend rage. But it's more exact to say that they pretend to pretend rage. Rage rages through them.

The Empty Vessel has been shifting without worry or thought. Material has been provided for them. They know what freely moving from experience to experience feels like. They're warmed up, ready for a solo flight.

6D. Solo Shifts

• One person gets up in front of the class. Choose either one, two, or three minutes within which you will perform the "shift" process. No director tells you when to shift, the choices are up to you. Do what feels right.

• Students in the audience pass along a watch taking turns being timer. After the designated period, the timer says, "Stop." There's no discussion between the solos. When they are all complete, students share their experiences with one another.

Performance

Not everyone in these training groups is interested in performance. At least, not in the beginning. Often when **Solo Shifts** is announced, a shudder of terror passes through the room.

Speaking in public is a common fear in just about all cultures. And **Solo Shifts** isn't just speaking. It's moving, too, and making sounds from the throat, from the body, from inside. But even beyond that, students present their vulnerability—their feelings.

After **Empty Vessel**, students are primed for a solo flight. They have been "**shifted**" by the messengers. The experience of radically changing from one mind set to another is in their bodies. They know what it feels like. They've experienced the cues embedded in the approximations. They're greased and ready to roll. The only problem is their thoughts.

I was eighth in line. I was glad I wasn't first and glad I wasn't the last either. I don't think I could have withstood the waiting and planning and then trying not to plan. As I watched the first seven solos, I saw many things that I was not going to do. And I thought about a few things that I was going to do. Like be calm. And simple. And direct myself to the audience. But when my turn came, and I stood up in front of the others for the first time, all of my plans vanished. I don't even remember breathing. I pretty much lost consciousness. I mean, I was conscious, but hysterical at the same time. Out of control. Out of my body. Thinking all the time and not getting anywhere. What should I do? Now, I understand rabbits when they freeze in front of oncoming headlights.

After forever, my time was up. I sat down feeling flushed and ashamed. I looked straight ahead. It wasn't until the next person was into their solo that I came back into my body and into the room.

Performance has many meanings, but the meanings take on new intensity when in front of a group. The experience enlarges. There's more at stake, or so we think. The performer is likely to be concerned with self-image and how others see them. "Am I doing this correctly?" "Will I have enough time to develop an idea?" "Will people think I'm good, or hopelessly inept?"

Those initially not interested in performance, begin to see it as more than what they thought it was. The freeing situation of it becomes a challenge in its own right—a metaphor for all the difficulties in life, all detours to inner stability, all "no's" ever encountered, and all moments of self-doubt.

Ruts

"I'm so tired of myself."
"I keep doing the same things."
"How do I get out of this rut of repetition?"

If a familiar quality of action, feeling, or even character continually presents itself to you, there's a reason. More than likely, you've not fully experienced it. A part of you stays in reserve, holds back, is afraid. The next time the familiar condition appears, approach it with detailed interest. Examine it. Then, give yourself wholeheartedly to the expression of the details. No holds barred. You will see that: 1) the experience is not what you expected, and 2) the condition will never reappear the same way again.

Thea had been trained as a dancer. She had a very specific style to her movements. In fact, the same movements appeared over and over again no matter what the context. As she became more aware of her patterns, she became very frustrated. She was at a loss as to how to go beyond them. Standing in front of the class, she was asked to execute a familiar move. When she did, everyone laughed, including her, probably from relief. That move was finally out in the open and identified. She was asked to execute the movement again and notice a particular detail about it. She was instructed to change the tension of the detail and play with it. Follow it along. Connect to the movement with feeling. This event gave Thea clues to the physical freedom which only lies in each moment.

6E. Performance Score: Back to Front, Silent

• Four people stand, side by side, in front of the audience with their backs to the audience. All you can do is turn, either to face the audience or to turn away from the audience. That's all. However, you can vary the speed of the turn and the amount of time you spend facing the audience. Most importantly, you and your partners play off each other's actions. Respond to each other's timing, energy, and intentions of actions. Don't look directly at each other. Feel each other. Your actions together create rhythmic patterns, music. Use peripheral vision and awareness. Trust your intuition about the others.

Pretending to Pretend

Jack, Jill, Jane and Jim stand with their backs to the rest of the audience. They stand still for a few moments, then Jack turns abruptly around and faces the audience. After a moment, Jill begins to turn, extremely slowly, toward the audience. There is tension on Jack's face. The audience is in suspense. Even though he's facing front, his expression tells us that he's listening to the movements of his partners. Jill continues to slowly turn. Jim abruptly turns to the front. Audience: giggles. His expression is also alert. Jack and Jim let the audience know that they are aware of being connected by this experience of facing front. Jill is still slowly turning. Jane abruptly turns to face the audience. She's listening, too. Jack, Jim and Jane know Jill is still turning and that she is taking a very long time. They indicate that to the audience through body tension and eyes. They wait. And so does the audience. Suddenly, Jill snaps the end of her turn and abruptly joins the others facing the audience. Silence. Immediately, Jack, Jim and Jane relax and still facing front, shift their eyes toward Jill. So does the audience. Jill looks enthusiastic. She's joined the gang. Now, she, alone, holds the tension. The audience laughs.

Back to Front/Silent is similar to **Three on a Bench,** relief from the complexities of the previous exercises. The brain can cool out. The participants only have a few choices, yet within those choices lie vast possibilities of experience. The situation of turning back and to front, metaphorically, captures much of being human and being human in relationship to other humans.

Within these constraints, humor often erupts. The relationships turn out to be about waiting, competing, challenging, tricking, being tricked, making friends, becoming adversaries, and being included or excluded. And on top of all of this is the absurdity of turning back and forth.

The exercises on Day Six ask the students to disengage from the clutter they place between themselves and their experience. When the constricting material of their personalities disappears, what's left is a feeling, sensing energy, a transparent vehicle for experiencing. The audience engages with the experience, not the experiencer. Both performer and audience meet in transparency.

The Body of Language

7A. Body Parts Move on Out-Breath
7B. Narrative on Beat
7C. Narrative with Varied Timing
7D. Language and Movement/Interruption
7E. Performance Score: Seated Dialogues

"Text" is a body of words.

"Narrative" is the vocal expression of a text.

To narrate is to speak text. A single text may be narrated in many different ways.

In Action Theater, we arrive at text through improvisation. Nothing is written down or memorized. Language is discovered in the walk backwards. We prepare for language by centering on the body and its breath.

Today, we focus on language and its relationship to the body. Students are reminded that the body talks. Talk talks. Not metaphorically, romantically or poetically, but, really and truly. If the student were to relax and become internally quiet, the body's voice would arise. The direct experience of language would happen without the mediation of the talker.

Before we jump into language, we settle into our bodies and listen to it speak.

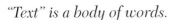

7A. Body Parts Move on Out-Breath

• Everyone, stand still in a comfortable position. Watch your breath. The air comes in, bounces out, and then there's a pause. Put your mind on a particular place in your body that relates to your breath, a small place, at the base of your nose, your diaphragm, or your abdomen. Experience the movement breath creates as it comes in, bounces out, and pauses. Watch the sensation of breath for the next five, or six, breaths.

• Begin to move just on each exhalation of each breath. When you inhale, be still. Start with your head. As you exhale, move your head only. The rest of you, your neck, your shoulders, etc., remain still. As you inhale, don't move at all . . . Add your left arm. Only on the exhalation. Move your head and your left arm. Add your right arm. Add your torso. And, now your legs. Every time you exhale, your whole body is in motion, and you're changing location.

• Play with re-ordering your breath. Make it percussive. Prolonged. Pants. Swirls. Etc.

• Get involved with what you're doing. Feel it. Be it.

• Now, within the next few minutes, become aware of somebody else in the room. Slowly begin to connect with them. Continue to move on only the out-breath in relation to one another.

An unvoiced exhalation has a vastness: a breath may be long or short, heavy or light, and be exhaled in various textures. An unvoiced exhalation may slide, gag, rasp, and sputter. It may sound hollow, tight, faint or mighty. Since language rides on the out-breath, it, like breath, has vast possibilities for design. The longer your out-breath exhalation is, the more space you will have to work with this. Practice making your out-breath last as long as possible before you take a breath in.

Present Pause

Whether we move or speak, we pause. "Pause" is different than "freeze." When a student freezes, he becomes immobile, static, both physically and psychically. When a performer pauses, he becomes physically immobile. Psychically, he is moving along, experiencing the ever-changing events inside and around him.

We're afraid to stop producing material. We think that not doing anything is "not being anything." We mis-interpret a pause as dead space and, so, once within in it, we tend to panic, become inert: we leave the present and we leave our bodies. We lose track of what's going on around us, and just stand around, observe, think we're invisible, mouth the words someone else is saying (unconsciously), and may get more and more tense without being aware if it. We suffer.

The alternative is to experience a pause as an expression of present attentiveness. Action stops so that listening can occur. Pause is an action that transmits information through its details: its muscular tension, gaze of the eyes, and quality of energy emanating from the body. Students talk to each other with actions and pauses. They can experiment further by minimizing action and emphasizing pauses.

A performer can let the audience know whether they are listening to something, thinking about something, feeling something, wanting something, afraid of something, etc., through the quality of their pause.

When partnering, several dynamics may arise. One is the phenomena of *connection*, when one or more partners are empathetic to the other. Another is *countering* or *blocking*, when one or more partners alters or inhibits the actions of the other.

Connect

Students are asked to "connect" with a partner. What does that mean?

> *Imagine you're sitting next to a stranger on the bus. All of his thoughts, feelings, actions, and dreams are available to you in your awareness. You'd notice him differently, wouldn't you? He would move. You'd "feel" it. He would speak. You'd "feel" it. He doesn't know you're even there. He's reading the newspaper. You don't need him to know you're there for you to experience him, to connect with him.*
>
> *On the other hand, suppose I knock on a door and a man answers the door and I put out my hand to shake his hand and he slams the door in my face and I go back the next day and I knock on the door and the man opens the door and I put out my hand to shake his and he slams the door in my face and I go back the next day and I knock on the door and the man opens the door and I put out my hand to shake his and he slams the door in my face. Would you call this a connection?*

Perhaps the person who knocked on the door was shocked by her reception and got caught in feelings of rejection. She was unable to notice

particulars about the person who slammed the door. She was blinded by her personal agenda. In this scenario, no connection was made.

But, if the knocker had no expectations, and made no judgments that would throw her into blinding emotion, she would have been able to notice the person slamming the door. After all, she had three opportunities. She would experience the reality of the person being annoyed by answering the door. She would, then, also feel her connection to his condition and understand the occurrence.

Suppose I am connecting to my partner and I become aware of myself judging my partner's actions. This is only a problem if I judge the judgment: if I feel shame, or am angry at her, or worry that the improvisation's not working. Alternately, I can recognize my judging as simply an OK thought, not better or worse than anything else. I can either let it go, or enter into it directly, become that judge, and bring that judgment into the action. If there's no judgments about judgments, I've remained connected to myself and to my partner.

Countering or Blocking

Countering or **Blocking** is when one performer's actions prevent, inhibit or attempt to control the actions of another. The most common examples in language are: "No," or "Stop," "Calm down," or "Shh," or "You don't mean that." Physically restraining somebody or stopping their movement is blocking.

Countering is a substitute for connecting to yourself. It's a manipulative action; "I don't have anything going on with myself, so I'm going to mess with what you have going on," or, "What you're doing scares me, so I'm going to stop it."

Some other countering methods are:

Using given names: When we call a person by his real name, it pulls him out of his fantasy and out of the improvisation. Instead, generate a name that's appropriate for the situation.

Using questions: Questions shift the attention and responsibility onto others. It's more constructive, and less alienating, to say the statement behind the question, or makeup the information the question seeks. In that way, you're promoting the improvisation, instead of draining it.

Commenting on the experience of self or partner: Objective, analytical, descriptive statements that come from outside of experience and carry with them no feeling, nor image, halt the lively flow of an improvisation. The problem isn't with the information, it's where it's coming from. The speaker is not involved in the experience. Instead, they're observing it. Their energy is flat and self-conscious.

Jon is sitting in the middle of the room, rocking back and forth on his feet, singing to himself. James walks over and says, "Looks like you're having fun."

If James' intention is solely to remark on John's situation, then he's commenting. If his intention is to indicate his inner condition, and his presentation does so, then it's not commenting.

Students are instructed to avoid all countering devices. They must accept everything their partner says or does. This challenges their self-imposed limits and forces them to be flexible. Later, when students have learned to not expect or depend on results, they may experiment with countering or blocking actions. Then countering or blocking actions are inroads and expressions of their own psyches.

Now, we approach language. Students build a narrative together being careful to accept everything each other has said.

7B. Narrative on Beat

• Everyone walk. Let's walk on the same regular beat. We're going to create a narrative together, a story with each one of us adding a segment. We're not going for a linear, rational story with a beginning, middle and end. Our narrative will unfold piece by piece, as we let our minds meander into dream world.

• You'll say a word, or a syllable, on every step and you'll speak for two or three minutes. You may repeat words, or syllables, as needed, particularly if the next word doesn't come to you in time for the next step. Feel the beat. Hear the beat. Listen to the unfolding narration. Put yourself inside it. Believe it.

• When you're ready to relinquish your turn, tap someone on the shoulder and, then, step off the floor. They pick up the very next step (or beat) with a word, or syllable, and continue the narrative. When they want to relinquish their turn, they'll tap someone. Eventually, everyone gets a turn.

• Speak loudly and clearly so you can be easily heard. Listen attentively to each other, so that if you are tapped, you'll know what you're coming into.

• The last remaining person on the floor concludes the narrative.

• I'll start us off.

Anyone who mastered hopscotch has no trouble with this exercise. Hopscotchers knew how to handle speech, movement, time and sometimes, even melody, all at the same time. The difference, here, is that the "stepper" is improvising the text. As with hopscotch, the less thought, the better.

This walking/talking exercise approaches language and the body similarly to the way sound and movement was approached on Day Two—as two aspects of a single expression. In this case, when there's speech, there's movement (stepping) and when there's movement, there's speech. A lot of balls in the air.

This lays some ground for speaking from the body. A conscious effort, again and again, of aligning speech and movement will, eventually, access an organic order.

The "beat" is incessant and the person taking up speaking and stepping knows that some utterance must appear on every step. There's no time for planning. What comes, comes as a surprise.

7C. Narrative with Varied Timing

Again, let's walk, with a word or syllable on every step. We'll begin by standing still. I'll start a different narration and, this time, I'll fill the language with feeling, texture. My language will vary in speed and energy depending on the feelings behind the words. Even though I'm continuing to put a step to every word or syllable, the timing and quality of the steps will constantly be changing.

Everyone else walks at the same time as the speaker and with the same energy. Don't look at the speaker. Listen.

When I want to relinquish my turn, I'll tap someone on the shoulder and leave the floor. We'll progress until everyone in the group has had a turn and left the floor.

Remember to pause as often as you like, for as long as you want.

Narrative

If you haven't told a story to a three-year-old, try it. This is an ideal test. If they stop listening and wonder off, more than likely, you've flattened, become dull, dry, lifeless. You've lost contact with your little listener. Children are drawn to contrast, the rise and fall of energy, change of pitch, surprise, tension, heightened drama, scary and funny things.

Because students step with the same energy as their words, they experience the dynamics of language as motion. Just as a dance may, or may not, elicit feeling, so language may, or may not, elicit feeling—depending upon its presentation.

Usually, speech is used to get an idea, or prospective, across. We focus on the content, talking towards the thought that lays ahead. In **Narrative with Varied Timing**, students play with each moment of speech and bring speech into present time.

Because they step with their words, students experience language as a moment-to-moment action. They make choices about each word, and every part of each word. They begin to dismantle their vocal conventions. They slow down to fill each moment with texture and feeling. Details get across. One sentence can carry a main idea, sub-ideas, and hints of other ideas. A sentence may carry one or more feelings that may even be contradictory.

Say these lines and play around with feeling and inflection. (Their page layout suggests different readings; the spaces between words might represent breaths, for instance.)

> *I want   to   touch   you.*
> *I want   to touch you.*
> *I   want to touch   you.*
> *I   want   to touch   you.*
> *I   want to touch you.*

In performance, the content of the words is only one part of the meaning. The flesh and spirit that we bring to these words complete the picture. The combination of flesh (body), spirit (feeling) and language (content) create meaning.

The song sparrows in Union Square, in San Francisco, share the same song as the song sparrows in The Mission District, only a few miles away. However, they each adhere to a dialect that is indigenous to their region.

Our speech incorporates patterns of tone and inflection depending on where and how we live. It's not that we want to erase our idiosyncrasies, it's that we want to know them. Idiosyncrasies suggest undiscovered expression. If we become conscious of a language quirk, the next time we experience that quirk, we can note its aspects and details. We can explore the details by amplifying, re-toning, re-timing, or contrasting. Once these details become conscious, we're no longer deafly bound.

7D. Language and Movement/Interruption

• In trios, you and your partners build a physical narrative, putting movement and text together. You're free to do any movement that you feel is appropriate to what you're saying. You're no longer limited to stepping.

• Begin from neutral stillness. One of you starts by moving and talking at the same time. Whenever you're active, you're active with language and movement. They're done as one action: the movement and the language are precisely concordant in time, duration, feeling and dynamic. When you're not talking, you're not moving, and vice-versa. Imagine that your body is doing the talking and your talking is doing the body. A loop of inspiration.

• You can fill the spaces with movement and speech, or pause. You can repeat yourself, play with a word or an idea. You can repeat your partner's actions and language, or add on from where they left off. Don't feel that you have to jam a lot of information into a small space. There's nowhere to go except where you are. Make the most of it and be the most of it.

• The space is yours until you get interrupted by one of your partners. When you're interrupted, stop immediately, even if it's in the middle of an action. Don't return to neutral, but stay where you are, whatever position and shape. Don't blank out. Stay aware of your partners.

• Partners, listen to each other. What you hear affects what you say and how you say it. Play off each other's timing. Orchestrate, hear the beats. Be aware of each other's physical shaping and shape in response to that awareness.

• Keep your interruptions erratic. Who interrupts, when they do so, and the duration between interruptions is unpredictable.

This exercise is a more evolved version of **Verbs Only** introduced in Day Five. Again, students put movement and language together, continuing the practice of integrating body/mind awareness. Here the students are not limited by saying what they're doing. They are free to build text from their imagination. Their physical actions reflect their relationship to that text.

What kind of movement is relevant to language?

There are three choices.

MIMETIC

The simplest and most direct is *mimetic* movement, movement that literally interprets the text. The speaker says, "Tree," and forms a tree with her body.

SUBTEXTUAL

Another choice reflects what we call *subtext:* information of emotion, or feeling, that concurrently lies unspoken beneath the spoken. The speaker says, "Tree," while sensually stroking herself, signifying some personal reality relative to "tree."

ASSOCIATIVE

Another choice is *associative movement* that reflects a different idea, or image. Here, the speaker says, "Tree," while simultaneously tearing paper. Associative actions may stray far from the content of the actual text. Whether the movements are sub-textual, or associative, what remains important is that the mover experiences coherency. Their verbal and physical images stick together.

The last two choices offer a broader scope of information from which to make meaning. Since the verbal and the physical images don't directly reinforce each other, the audience experiences a wholeness that is beyond the sum of the parts.

Blocked/Stuck/Empty

What do you say when you don't know what to say?

Again, there are some choices. One is to come to terms with your speechlessness and speak about it. For example:

> *"I would say something if I knew what to say."*
> *"I have nothing to say about . . ."*
> *"I'm afraid if I say something it might be wrong . . . and you will think . . . and then I will have to"*
> *"I need some silence to think."*
> *"Wait, I'm thinking."*
> *"I'm hot, in a panic and can't talk."*
> *"I'm not moving—speaking—frozen—paralyzed . . ."*
> *And on and on.*

Obviously, if you get yourself to the point of talking about not talking, you're talking. You've slipped out of speechlessness and into speech. But, it's not always that easy. Consciousness must be brought into the experience of speechlessness, and for some people that, in itself, is an arduous task. Sometimes, just experiencing an unconscious freeze, over and over again, leads to conscious recognition. Side-coaching from a teacher, or an observing partner often helps: "Where are you right now?" A question from the outside may jar the student, and wake him up to his state. Once recognition occurs, the change has begun. The experience can be observed. Objectivity and detachment can come into play. An observed experience is diffused of the power to strangle and gag. The observer has taken charge. He can interact with the condition of speechlessness and mine it for riches.

Another choice is to copy what one of your partners says. If you can't think of anything to say, then don't *think*, simply say exactly what another person is saying—maybe even try to do it at the same time. "**Empty Vessel**" them, so to speak. This approach often activates an energy flow and the previously stuck speaker can take off.

An even more sophisticated approach would be to build a metaphoric, or fantastic, narrative using present feelings as a base. For example:

> *Sabine is feeling confused. She isn't clear what her partners are talking about and doesn't know how to fit in. Sabine notices this experience. She talks about an orphan who comes upon a strange village. The orphan doesn't know how to fit in. The orphan's confused, can't get clear what people are talking about. She goes from person to person trying to find shelter. The story builds from there and Sabine's home free.*

We're not making theater about robots who always have the perfect things to say, the perfect gestures to make and are perfect. We're making theater about people who have all kinds of experiences: some flow; some are light, humorous, deep, profound; some are about confusion, stuck-ness, stupidity, fear, anger and other perfect imperfections. This is theater of people.

7E. Performance Score: Seated Dialogues

• Two or three of you sit in chairs facing out toward the rest of the class, turned slightly toward each other. Have a dialogue, a conversation. Talk about anything. Be simple. Really listen to each other. Take what each other says seriously. Believe it. And listen to yourself and believe that. Be with each part of each word as you speak it. Play with pauses and hold tension in them. Hear the way your partners speak words, their timing, pitches, quality of energy. When you speak, follow through with the sound patterns as you hear them, or break patterns and create surprises.

The Sound Of Language

This exercise is the introduction to dialogue. We enter dialogue by listening. To simplify the task, we de-emphasize content. We keep it simple. Dialogue tends to trap us in mundane, ordinary, and dependent relationships. We bog down and get lost in our own and another's agenda. Listening prevents this from happening. By listening, we create music together with the spoken word. A simple example of a musical dialogue follows. Notice the patterns and rhythm. Imagine the rise and fall of inflection and pauses.

> *"Hello."*
> *"Hello."*
> *"I haven't seen you in a long time."*
> *"Yes."*
> *"You're looking well."*
> *"Yes."*
> *"Healthy."*
> *"Yes. I've been away."*
> *"Really."*
> *"In Germany."*

"Really."
"Yes, for a year."
"Really. I have family there."
"Really."

If we can let just sound inspire, we can free ourselves from the absorption in content. The sound of speech furthers the sounds of speech. Whatever one partner says to another is perfect. Everything they say, or do, is accepted. Nothing is denied or countered. We adapt, flex, change, and shift perspective to further the music, to satisfy our listening.

Day Seven tuned the ear to hear the present, the music of spoken language. As our capability to listen increases, the students' need to speak particular ideas at particular times lessens. This in turn allows more room for a choice of utterance and silence.

Transformation

8A. One Sounder, All Move
8B. Facings and Placings
8C. Transform Content, Movement Only
8D. Transform Content, Sound and Movement
8E. Transform Content, Phrase and Gesture
8F. Performance Score: One-Upping

The dog chews its tail. What started as a nibble at a flea bite has become a dance, a ritual, tantalizing, familiar, repeated over and over again, yet each time, brand new. It's not a matter of outcome. Round and round, the dog stabs, gnashes and thrusts, and each stab inspires another and another gnash leads to another thrust. One move inspires the next and the next responds to the one before. The frenzy of the dog becomes more significant than the causes of his motion.

We are not the act. The act moves us. Our awareness keeps the act from overwhelming us. The next exercise invites students to be moved to their fullest capacity while maintaining awareness.

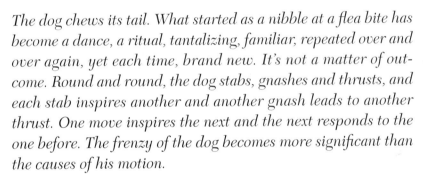

8A. One Sounder, All Move

• Find a place for yourself in the room and stand still, eyes open. Bring your attention to your breath. Release any tension that you're aware of, in your body or mind. As you watch your breath come in and go out, find an inner stillness.

• I'm going to vocalize. I will make sounds for three to five minutes. My sounds will both inspire and reflect an inner journey. The sounds will create the journey and that journey will have an affect on the sounds.

• You're all movers. Respond to my sounds. Don't mirror them. Contrast what you hear to what you do, in timing, texture and feeling.

• After three to five minutes, I will pass on the position of sounder to someone else by going over to a mover (while I'm still sounding) and assuming their physical expression. That mover, then, takes on my sounds. We trade places. The new sounder goes off the floor, to the side of the room, and sounds on his/her own for three to five minutes, before passing her sounds onto a new sounder.

• While the third or fourth sounder vocalizes, begin to connect with one another, in duets and trios. Respond to what you hear, your inner impulses, what your partners are doing, and your experience of them. You must be still some of the time so that you can listen to all these things.

• We'll continue this until everyone has had a turn as sounder. The last sounder will bring her sounds to a close to end the exercise.

$$\smallsmile \ \bullet$$

Against the Beat

Sound often dominates the actions of the mover. We're drawn to move to the beat of sound, maybe, because of the drumming of our hearts, the old familiar two-step, cheering on with our cheerleaders or rock and rolling. To not move to the beat requires a shift of attention to listening. One's inner music, carrying its own timing and rhythm, shares the foreground. The counterpoint tension between inner and outer timing leads the student into an alarming, alert and awakened field.

Eli is almost two months old. He likes wrap-around-sound. Music, the clothes dryer, the vacuum cleaner. He relaxes, lays back and floats.

In order to float, we must relax. The sound will enter our body. It will touch an early place, an "Eli" place, and we, too, will float.

The exercises in this training may seem to lead to opposite directions. On the one hand, we talk about floating, letting go of the ourselves and relaxing into direct experience. On the other, we practice techniques of control, awareness, composition, form. Yes and yes, to both. The latter develops craft and the former expands the possibilities of what we experience directly.

8B. Facings and Placings

• Everyone, stand somewhere on the floor. Change the direction that you're facing . . . change your facing again . . . again . . . change your location . . . change your location and facing . . . just change your location . . . change your shape . . . change your shape and location . . . change your shape, location, and facing . . . just your shape . . . just facing . . . change your shape and level (for instance, lying on the floor for the low range, standing, or reaching, for the upper range and sitting, or kneeling, for the mid-range, etc.) . . . change your shape, level, facing and location . . . change the tension only . . . change the tension again . . . change the shape, level and tension . . .

• Put yourself into small groups, trios or quartets. Stand in "neutral" together. From this position, begin an improvisation together in which you only move from placement to placement, fairly percussively. Every time you move, change your facing, shape, level, location, tension, or any combination of those. Be in relationship with your partners.

• Fill your forms with feeling, intention, meaning. Play off each others' timing as well. You will be responding to your partners with every choice you make.

＼＿ •

Space and Shape

On the first day of the training, students became aware of timing. On another, they became aware of shape. On a successive day, they studied pauses. On another day, they focused on intention. They're accumulating skills that affect everything they do. Nothing is forgotten nor left behind. For example, the previous exercise, **Facings and Placings** calls for alertness to timing, contrast, attentiveness to one's partner, gathering information, and filling form with feeling and intention. Students are learning to twine a braid of skills; the braid doesn't simply get longer, it gets fatter.

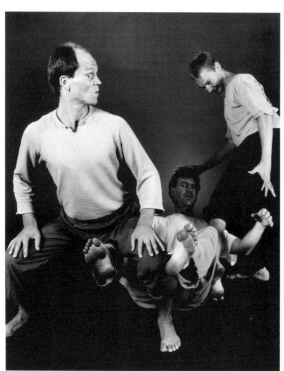

As they practice a skill, again and again (timing, for instance), their awareness expands to include more detail, nuances and subtleties. As "timing" becomes more articulated, they experience more, which leads, again, to a broader landscape of experience.

To see how placement affects meaning, visualize the following different situations.

Two women facing front, in the middle of the room, standing side by side.

Two women at the back wall, standing side by side, and facing the back wall.

One woman standing in the

*center of the room facing front, the other standing in the right
rear corner facing the right wall.*

*One woman kneeling facing front in the right rear corner, the
other in the left corner, kneeling, facing front.*

*Two women, one kneeling in the center of the back wall fac-
ing front, the other standing facing front in the right front corner.*

*Two women, one standing in the center of the room, the other
kneeling towards the back wall in the left rear corner.*

*Two women standing side by side in the center of the room,
facing front.*

*Two women standing in the center of the room facing front,
one half-way behind the other.*

Where we place an action, how we locate it in space, affects its meaning. Location determines perspective and perspective affects power. The
women in the images above, were described as only standing or kneeling. No expression, or other activity, was given. But if we were to visualize these scenes, our imagination would respond to the emptiness and
fill it with story. A woman folded in the corner, back to audience, or a
woman folded stage center, front to audience, are quite different images;
they elicit very different feelings.

Dynamics

Dynamics refers to the force of an action: the combined phenomena of
time and energy. When we say, "Change the tension," we're reconfigur-
ing time and energy dynamics. Changing the dynamic of an action, is
another way to tamper with its meaning.

*Slowly, turn your head from side to side in a relaxed fashion. Add
tension to that action. Now, add speed. Notice how the inner experience of your head turning changes. How do your feelings respond
to the variations?*

*Try this with language. Say a phrase and then vary the tim-
ing and tension. What happens?*

Here, we're purposefully manipulating the dynamics of our actions so that we can experience ranges we may not normally reach. After enough practice, we can stop bothering to make it so hard. A range of dynamics will become part of our expressive language, ready to respond to our inner experience.

Transformation

A leaf slowly turns brown. Drying out, it becomes dark and crisp. Nothing wet anymore, nothing to hold it to the tree. It drops to the ground, shrinks, becomes darker and drier. Nothing to hold it to itself. It breaks into small pieces, becoming powder, becoming earth. Is it still a leaf? Is earth leaf and leaf earth?

The leaf changes, becoming different in consistency, but more of itself. We could say, "Fulfilling its destiny." We could say that the transformation exercises in this training are practices that teach us how to begin to fulfill destiny.

On Day Three, we introduced the reader to the process of **shift, transform,** and **develop.** So far, the exercises have concentrated on **shift** and the **development** that happens between each shift. Now, we complete the triad. We move into **transformation,** the process of incremental changes which are visually seen and bodily felt.

◄ •

8C. Transform Content, Movement Only

• In pairs. One of you will be Watcher and the other, Doer. Watcher, assign a simple physical gesture to the Doer. For example, a clap of the hands, a touch to the forehead, or a turn of the body while lifting two hands. The gesture is an "empty" form with no emotional or attitudinal fill. Be sure the gesture has a beginning and an end. Then, step aside and prepare to watch.

• Doer, with regular timing, continually repeat the shape of the gesture given to you exactly the way it was given to you. Begin with a few "empty" repetitions. Keep repeating it on a pulse. Become familiar with the movement so you don't have to think about it later. Then, connect your imagination and feelings to your actions. Fill the gesture.

• Now, each time you repeat the gesture, incrementally change your mind/body. One state inspires the next, so you're transforming the meaning of the action step by step. Between each step, empty out the meaning so a clear beginning and end to the action can be seen. The movement may slow down, or speed up, or the muscles around the bones may change tension in order to respond to your changing internal experience. The shape of your skeleton and the pulse of your action, however, should remain the same.

• Remember, one gesture leads you to the next. Don't think up your moves. Each repeat is a slight change, physically and psychically, in the direction that you're already heading. You're transforming the content of the action, nothing else.

• How do you know where you're heading? Signs and arrows point the way. While you're executing the action, be aware of the sensations you experience, both physically and psychically, in detail. Those sensory details are the signs and arrows that point in the direction of your next move.

• Each time you repeat the form, go one step farther than where you've just been. This doesn't have to mean bigger and louder. Let go of plans and follow the details of the experience. Go into the realm of non-understanding.

• Watcher, if you notice that your partner jumps a step—indicating that they're thinking ahead—or repeats the content, or vacillates back and forth between hard/soft, stop them. Put them back on track. Remind them to watch the details and follow those details, increment by increment. No mental work. A direct line, from awareness to action to awareness.

We begin each transformation exercise with an empty form. The word "empty" is another covenant. For us, it means: a movement form devoid of as much content as possible. No "I" is in the action. It is defined only by the body with no mind state informing its meaning. We say "empty" even though we know that nothing is empty. Emptiness is emptiness, emptiness is itself. Even an empty gesture is full of its own emptiness.

Students perform these transformational explorations with regular pulse. The pulse keeps the student transforming and doesn't give her time to drift into thought, or slide into repetition or trance. With this regular pulse, students must constantly track their experience: mental and physical sensations, shapes that pass though body and mind. They respond to each sensation as it occurs and from where it begins and ends.

Transformation is an evolutionary process. Each step on the way is like a fossil in an evolutionary chain from point A to point B. There's no missing link. It's a smooth flow. Unlike a shift, where some miracle brings the person from one state to another, a transformation leaves a trail of residue indicating how one action became the next. The change in shape, intention, energy, time, and facial expression can be traced back to the shift before. A transformation is essentially one tiny shift after another, but we look at it over a whole path to see the gradual change take place. Shifts leave no tracks. Nothing exist from A to B. There's no evidence of how one led to the next.

What are the cues that suggest the next action and how can they be detected? Here is an example:

> *I'm standing up. I clap my hands together. I notice a bounciness on the release of the clap. The next time I repeat the clap, I give more attention to the bounciness and I notice that along with the bounciness is a lightness of spirit. The next time I repeat the clap, I move more into the bounciness and the light spirit, and I notice a tension arising in both the inward and outward action of the clap, running up my arms into my neck and face. The next time I repeat the clap, I move more into the tension and notice that my facial and neck muscles are pulling back and my entire body is tightening. I feel my spirit contracting. The next time I repeat the clap I move more into the physical tension and tightness of*

that spirit and I notice my eyebrows lifting, my eyes bulging, my breath holding and an even tighter, and now, expansive quality to my spirit. The next time I repeat the clap, I move more into tightness and expansiveness and I notice that at the end of the clap my fingers are curving slightly, and along with that curving is a slight release of tension, and a subtle retreating of spirit. The next time I repeat the clap, I move more into that curve, the release of tension and the retreating and I notice my chest is collapsing and my shoulders are turning inward, my fingers are feeling light and formless and my spirit is softening . . .

This process precludes any "happy, happier, happiest," or the "little girl, bride, old lady" tactics. There's no time or space for imaging or planning. No pre-thought, no identifications. Stereotyped images tug us away from present moment and our own body. They are externalized images which require thinking, analyzing. Thinking interrupts the lively ongoing-ness of the body. Analysis is not movement from within, and can't be the motivation of our action. We sense this difference.

Again, students walk backwards into direct experiencing, noticing and following the cues in their current mind/body, allowing their actions to take them into unpredictable and unnameable terrains.

Now we add variables.

8D. Transform Content, Sound and Movement

• Everyone, change partners. We'll repeat the previous exercise. This time, we'll work with a sound and movement gesture. The transformation will occur within the conjunction of the sound, movement and intention of the action. Just as the bones of the movement remain constant, so do the bones of the sound, (the bones being the shaping of the sound in the mouth). For example, if the sound is a "ba" sound, it doesn't transform into a "fa" sound. It stays a "ba" sound, but the tension, volume and speed of that "ba" sound transforms just as the quality of the movement transforms.

8E. Transform Content, Phrase and Gesture

• Change partners and we'll repeat the previous exercise. However, this time each of you will assign a combined phrase and gesture to the other. As you transform the action, have the phrase and gesture ride simultaneously just as a sound and movement would. If there's no movement, then there's no sound, and if there's no sound, there's no movement. Again language, movement and intention transform simultaneously.

To perform this exercise, students must, as in earlier language exercises, detach, in part, from the meaning of the language. They must "hear" its sound and "feel" the kinetics, as well as know the meaning. Then, as they transform the phrase and gesture, they're free to stretch the articulation of their speech beyond what they normally would.

8F. Performance Score: One-Upping

• Two people go and stand out on the floor. Two people from the audience go out and each assign one of the performers a gesture and verbal phrase, in secret. Be sure that gesture and the language are synchronized in detail. Once you've made your assignment, come back and join the audience.

• The two performers, face off with a few feet between you, standing in neutral. Using only the material you've been given, and by alternating turns, you will collaborate on a transformation. One of you performs your action (phrase and gesture). The other immediately performs their action in response. Back and forth, no time in between. Each time it's your turn, repeat your action, but fill it with the energy, tension and intention of your partner, and go a little further. Each time pick up your partner's cues: details; articulation of energy; expression of the face, eyes; music, inflection and tone of the voice; timing and spirit. Use the same accents and rhythm even though your phrases are different. "Get out of my house!" will sound and feel the same as "Have you seen my comb?"

• Pay close attention to each other. You're both riding an endless current of energy. Responding and driving, responding and driving.

• If needed, I will side-coach you. If I find that you're either jumping ahead (by asserting something that was not indicated in your partner's action), repeating, or not listening and observing, I'll either throw in a comment to put you back on track, or stop you. Be in your ears, eyes, and body. Follow each other's sounds, energy, and spirit. Relax and get in a groove together.

＊

Students can always advance further into a territory than they think they can. They tend, unguided, to veer off into another direction before they challenge their capacity to hold, extend, and continue the progression into the current direction. It's not that students are unwilling. Until they're familiar with the experience of letting go into the unfamiliar, they often miss the jump off place. They're too busy doing the exercise, listening, and observing and doing, doing, doing. An encouraging voice from the outside (side-coaching) can help. "Further. Go further into that. What do you notice? Go with that. Even further. Focus. Go further. Further."

"Further" doesn't necessarily mean bigger and louder. The task is to follow the details as they lead into *any* body/mind state.

In **One-Upping**, each partner incited the other. One may have driven into an area that the other might normally avoid because it was dangerous or frightening. The partner had no choice but to follow, and go one increment further. They were on the train. The directions were clear. The side coach was there to support and guide. The audience was witness.

Each move in a transformation exercises is like one bead on a string of many gradually shaded colored beads. As we transform, we move from one bead to the next until we reach a completely new color, and then we keep going. If a bead is out of place, or a color deepens too quickly, we feel rupture in the order. Here, it is order that leads to the unpredictable.

Transformation calls for letting go. It insists that one remain within the experience of the body. One is safe within awareness. Eyes, ears, and body. Sensation. Spirit. Everything else disappears. No judgments or plans. No opinions, memories, fantasies. Only awareness. Only what you have here, within you, not your stories, background, dreams, desires, images. Just what happens in these moments. Only being in action. It's enough.

Imagination

9A. Body Parts Lead
9B. Non-Stop Talk
9C. Shape/Freeze/Language
9D. Two Shape/One Reads
9E. Two Shape/One Bumps and Talks
9F. Questioner/Narrator
9G. Performance Score: Five Chairs

Start with the smallest of the small, a fraction of a moment of a moment. Now. Or now. Describe it. What are you doing and how are you doing it? Notice the details. Describe them. Are you in motion or not? What's the tension like in different parts of your body? Where are you? In a room? Outside? Where are you in relation to the space, the room, or the out of doors, that you're in? Describe your environment. In detail. How is each part of your body shaped in relation to each other part? Describe the quality of energy in your body. What thoughts or images are occupying your attention? Do all parts of your body feel of equal temperature? What sounds are in your landscape?

Can you be involved with your experience while noticing your involvement?

Practice.

We begin the ninth day with movement. A simple and playful opener which brings together a collection of skills: balance, coordination, travelling through space, rhythm, physical awareness and control, awareness of others while moving quickly, and identifying and isolating parts of the body. The body learns these skills without any assistance from the analytical mind. If trusted, the body can be a quick learner. Therefore, we approach these exercises without discussion.

9A. Body Parts Lead

• I'll beat a drum in a regular rhythm. Everyone, step with every beat. Step, step, step, step, step . . . Now, lead with your head. Follow it as it travels around the room. Up, down, side to side, twists and turns. Your head has a mind of its own . . . Lead with your right arm. Follow your right arm around the room . . . Lead with your left arm. Follow your left arm . . . Your sternum . . . forward, backward, sideways, up, down and around, slow, fast, always changing as you step to the beat of the drum Big steps, wide steps, move into the open space of the room. Lead with your hips. Front, side, back. Step to the beat of the drum. Lead with your knees . . . Forward, sideways. And, now, your feet . . . your feet are in front of the rest of your body, no matter what direction you're going in. Step to the beat of the drum.

• For eight beats, lead with your head, the next eight, your right arm, eight with the left arm, eight with the sternum, eight with the hips, eight with the knees, eight with the feet . . . Now, on five counts. Five with the head, five with the right arm, left arm, etc. Four counts . . . Three counts . . . Two counts . . . One count. Head, right arm, left arm, sternum, hips, knees, feet. Dance it. Travel.

Occasionally, students mouth the counts as they move. "Head, 2,3,4, 5,6,7,8. . . . right shoulder, 2,3,4,5,6,7,8. . . . left shoulder, 2,3,4,5,6,7,8. . . ," over and over. As the progressions get faster and shorter, these students get more and more behind time and more and more frustrated. If they were to let go of counting, resting in the physical experience, and trusting their bodies to feel the count, at the early stages of the event, their body would learn the organization.

> *In a modern dance class, a teacher demonstrates a 32-count sequence of movements. As she demonstrates, some of the students observe through their bodies. Almost imperceptibly, their bodies move along with hers. They are the ones who are going to be able to memorize the combination. They are not thinking. They are trusting their bodies to learn the sequence. They don't count. Nor do they analyze the movements. They receive the new information directly from the teacher's body to their body. Body to body. Through years of practice, they've come to this kind of learning.*

Spirit

> *We hunt for treasure. We hunt for it and find it at the same time as we notice every aspect of our experience. We observe clues and see that everything is "clue" to now and onward. The clues are unfamiliar, mysterious. Today's crooked finger is not the same as yesterday's crooked finger. The pattern of the breath is not the same as before. We can't predict anything. We don't know anything. Each clue is a state of mind. The clue and the state of mind are one thing. The crooked finger feels its way into the mind and the mind feels its way into the crooked finger. The body and the mind are crooked finger. Unfamiliar, complete, uncovered spirit.*

As we discovered earlier in transformations, even small shifts of the body's alignment can affect the psyche. A thrust forward of the hips, or an inward turn of a foot. Because of doing this movement, one feels differently. The psyche responds to this different feeling. Not necessarily with image, story or inner dialogue. There's a quality, a condition, or a state of being that inhabits the entire organism. It's un-nameable, but we call it spirit.

Some students come into these trainings more prepared to express themselves through movement, others more through language. Dancers and actors are the most obvious examples. But, individual nature, combined with cultural and family conditioning, usually predisposes one way or another, particularly when it comes to accessing and giving voice to the imagination.

The following exercises approach the imagination a variety of ways.

⌣ •

9B. Non-Stop Talk

• Stand on the floor. Move as little as possible. Begin talking. And don't stop. Listen to yourself. Pay attention to what you're saying, no matter what it is. Follow your train of thought, or let your mind jump around. Whatever works. Keep talking. Even if you repeat yourself, continue talking, non-stop. Not fast. Just constant.

⌣ •

We don't have to think about grammar, or syntax, as we speak. We know our language. We're free to play with content, to lie, exaggerate, fantasize, or atrociously act out. We can disassociate from our logical, and learned, patterns of thought and free the untamed mind.

With this exercise, each moment is filled with words. If words are *listened* to without judgment, from an innocent belief that the word is true, the next word will come and ideas will follow. If the narrator, for one moment, distracts (*dis-tracks*) himself with self-criticism or judgment, or jumps ahead of where he is, the text will disappear, leaving a naked, awkward, self-conscious performer.

If one were learning lines in preparation for a role in a play, the task becomes easier if the actor stays *in* the scene and is alive to it. Even the task of learning lines becomes a body event.

We humans share mind quirkiness. Until we become skilled at quieting the mind, it will flicker and dart from object to object. It's our underbelly, the place we're soft and frail. We recognize each others' underbellies and resonate together in the domain of distraction. Most of what we think of as "funny," our comedy and jokes, pokes at these inner struggles and peculiarities.

Our texts will have more body, depth, humanity if we bring our whole selves forth. Layers of consciousness add depth and idiosyncrasies to experience. The trick is to be conscious and accept everything that comes: no matter what it is. Whether or not we choose to act on material as it surfaces is dependent on its relevancy to the moment, not fear of being exposed.

9C. Shape/Freeze/Language

• I'll call out words that describe ways of moving. You improvise movement that responds to these words. Connect with your movement. You're moving spirit as well as body. At some point I'll say "Freeze." Stop moving and connect your shape and spirit with your imagination. Who are you? What are you up to? What's your context or condition? In sequence, one at a time, and in full voice, call out who you are, what you are and what you know about yourself.

Straight lines . . . Freeze and speak
Jagged edges . . . Freeze and speak
Jumps . . . Freeze and speak
Twists and knots . . . freeze and speak
Heavy spaces, . . . freeze and speak
Erratic curves . . . freeze and speak
Etc.

Much of this training asks students not to identify their experience, not to call it anything, or put any kind of name or label on it. They're encouraged to stay with sensations from moment to moment, becoming comfortable with, and finally attracted to the unknown.

But, here, students are asked to make identifications. They're learning about language, about how they talk, and what they talk about.

Language is comprised of images. We want the images to come from the present condition of the body, not from dissociative thinking. Therefore, the student freezes, not just in a shape, but in a moment of being. Their inner condition is not yet a verbal experience. The next step is naming, verbalizing. They must do so quickly. They must not leave the body to search for a character, or situation. Instead, they let feelings and sensation reveal to them the image. The body tells them what its condition is.

> *A naked woman hauling a heavy sack up a hill.*
> *An eagle carrying a tiny baby.*
> *Tom banging on Josephine's door with a heavy bowl.*
> *A body floating in a black river.*
> *Lightning cracking a medieval castle.*
> *A woman possessed by fire.*
> *A nonchalant hipster kicking the library wall.*
> *An old man looking across the corn-field into the future.*

Where do these images come from?

As students relax into their imagination, more and more sources of experience become available to them. At first, they may choose the most obvious image, the first thing that comes to mind. On that level, twenty students looking at the same "freeze" might image the same thing. As their imagination expands, students are no longer content with predictable, or generic interpretation. They begin to delve into freer associations and combinations of events without time and space boundaries, without demarcations between ordinary and extraordinary, real and surreal, mythic and mundane.

9D. Two Shape/One Reads

• Arrange yourselves into trios. Person A steps out and takes the role of Reader. The other two will make scenes for the Reader to identify. First, B makes a shape with intention and expression and freezes. C adds on to B's scene with another intention-filled shape and freezes. Contact is not necessary, nor is adding a shape that directly relates. Hold your scene while the Reader names and describes their situation. When A completes a short synopsis, B and C break the scene. Then you build another, this time with C starting and B adding on. Again, A reads the scene.

• Continue this arrangement until I say stop. We'll do three sets of this exercise so that each of you has a turn as Reader.

The Power of the Non-Linear

Students are encouraged to construct non-linear scenes, to search out the unexpected. They're not to write plays or scenes as they shape, or anticipate the Reader. Without worrying about meaning, they impulsively build onto each other's scenes.

Here are some examples of the difference between linear and non-linear actions. Causality, action-reaction is missing in non-linear actions, as well as expected (clichéd and stereotyped) sequences.

Linear:

> *A stands with hands up* ⟶ *B points gun*
>
> *A cries* ⟶ *B comforts*
>
> *A stands at attention* ⟶ *B corrects A's posture*

Non-linear:

> *A stands with clenched fist* ⟶ *B lolls at A's feet smiling languidly with eyes rolled back*
>
> *A cries* ⟶ *B bangs nails into the floor*
>
> *A stands tensely, with arms outstretched* ⟶ *B fixes hair*

The two Shapers must find ways to visibly connect these non-linear sequences. Otherwise they will appear as if they have nothing to do with each other. They do this by indicating, primarily with their eye focus and with the detailed shape and space composition, that they are in direct response to each other. Just oddly.

The Reader must describe a scene that includes both images. The latter combinations above challenge the Reader's imagination. Non-linear shapes that don't complete each other's narrative require both the Reader's and Shaper's immediate, spontaneous attention. Everyone stretches their capacity to live with uncertainty.

9E. Two Shape/One Bumps and Talks

• Again in trios. And again, two shape and one reads. But in this case, instead of the Reader describing the scene from outside, the Reader bumps (replaces) one of the Shapers, assumes his situation (intention and shape) speaks from *inside* that role. He narrates the scene while inside it, giving clues as to who or what you both are, and what your relationship and situation is. You all end up being Readers at one time or another.

• This is done in round/robin sequence.

A freezes.
B adds on, freezes.
C bumps A and does the reading from inside.

B freezes.
C adds on, freezes.
A bumps B and reads from inside.

C freezes.
A adds on, freezes.
B bumps C and reads from inside.

A freezes.
B adds on, freezes.
C bumps A and reads from inside.

etc.

• Continue going until I say stop.

The Reader gives specific information from his view of the story. The more he believes the posture and condition he has assumed, the more flowing the narration. He doesn't have to think because the scene is not something outside of himself. He's in it. His assumed situation and condition has awareness of its own. It has body, energy, posture, voice and feeling. The voice the Reader uses is a manifestation of the energy and feeling. The voice has a particular texture, pattern of articulation, and timing.

Dialects

Students are asked to avoid dialects because they are imitative. The Irish brogue, Southern drawl, or any foreign accent all suggest that the student is attempting to talk a particular way, rather than access and express immediate aspects of themselves. Their speech becomes too "heady," comes too much from a thinking state, instead of a feeling one. Dialects, as a result, often turn into plans that abandon the present moment. Instead, patterns of speech should actually respond to the present embodied condition. The student is to focus on her moment-to-moment experience rather than an idea, image, or description of experience. The quality of the student's voice will reflect these moments.

Students may feel "blocked," or "pressured," because they think they need a complete idea of what they're about to say before they say it. However, they don't have to know their entire text before they start. Narrations may begin with just one word, "I," or "My," or "Take." It's much better to build, word upon word, sometimes very slowly, until the content takes hold, than to deliver an entirely prepared speech. One word at a time leads to more spontaneous images and associations. The interesting part is what happens as the story unfolds.

9F. Questioner/Narrator

• In pairs. One partner is the Narrator. The other is the Questioner. The Narrator begins with a simple image, for example, "A stairway," or "A beautiful woman." The Questioner, asks a question that leads to more information about the image. For example, in the case of the stairway, the question may be, "From where to where?" The Narrator answers accordingly. The Questioner asks another question and the Narrator answers.

• The Questioner does not intentionally lead the Narrator into new territory. Instead, each question should intend to explore what the Narrator has already implied. The Questioner must not lead by introducing any new elements.

• Continue this exchange until I say stop. Then you will switch roles.

Example:

Narrator	*"A stairway."*
Questioner	*"Leading from where?"*
Narrator	*"From the cellar to the kitchen."*
Questioner	*"What's the kitchen like?"*
Narrator	*"It's a 1950s kitchen with pale green tiles on the walls and counter tops and a grey linoleum floor."*
Questioner	*"Is the kitchen clean?"*
Narrator	*"The floor's very dirty. The entire kitchen's dirty. The sink's full of dirty dishes, there's food all over the place, open, exposed. The screen door's slamming."*
Questioner	*"Did someone just leave?"*

This last question is a leading one, since the Narrator didn't mention a "someone." A better question would be:

> Questioner   *"Why is the screen door slamming?"*

Co-Believing

The Questioner and Narrator link in fantasy, each one stepping into niches the other provides. They believe and take themselves seriously and they believe each other. In order to ask a question, the Questioner must listen intently to the Narrator's information. Unconditionally. The Narrator must take seriously the Questioner's questions and not get so involved that he forgets to answer them. The end product is a composite of their two intentions focused on the material at that moment in time. Both of them are led into territories they would not have ventured alone.

This exercise helps show students that everybody has access to an incredibly vast imagination. With each question, there is always an answer. There's no limit to the questions, or the answers.

In the final event of the day, everything comes together in an interactive score.

9G. Performance Score: Five Chairs

• I've made an arrangement of five seating possibilities. One of them is a pillow, one's a low chair. There's a couple of high chairs, and a stool. All different. Five people go and sit at these locations.

• Each of you will assume a being, or entity. Sit in a particular posture, carry a particular energy, have a particular voice and style of speaking. There's something going on with you and you're speaking from a particular situation. You're all in very different worlds and your realities are in high contrast to one another.

• This score has three sections.

• First: In sequence, one by one, take a few minutes to introduce yourselves (not necessarily by name nor directly to the audience), but by bringing us into the middle of your world at this moment.

• Second section: After you've each introduced yourselves, randomly alternate turns by interrupting each other. Anyone may talk at any time and the talking space is yours until you get interrupted. Each time you speak, pick up where you left off. Continue to develop your monologues without transforming either the form or the content. If you are speaking and you get interrupted, stop speaking, but hold onto the body and intent throughout your pause. Remember, these are monologues, not dialogues. Play with the timing of your interruptions. Don't draw, or bridge content, from each other. You're now collaborating on the musicality of your interaction. Speak out to the audience.

• Third section: You may leave your seat and move to another location. If no one's sitting in that chair, you may sit in it. If someone is, then you stand, or kneel, beside them. You assume the same being as who first inhabited that seat, the style of body, the condition of mind, voice and content. If there's

more than one of you there, then speak simultaneously. It's possible that all five of you may be hovering around one location, in which case you're all speaking as the same being.

Continue until I say, "Stop," or I may give you a one minute cue to find an ending.

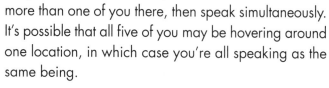

These five students are collaborating. They are co-designing the whole event, working with how it flows from one experience to another, whether the dynamics rise or flatten, what the voices sound like in relationship, how they dance together as they change location. They do this by listening to each other's sounds and sensing each other's movements. They use their instrument (body and voice) to respond to what they perceive. They amuse themselves within the context of each other.

A violin can have a voice. So can a dog, a diamond or water. Anything, if it resonates within a person's spirit, is fair game. Anything can act as vehicle through which the student finds herself. Each entity sitting in each chair is an invitation. The student either accepts the invitation, travelling within and beyond herself, or she doesn't. She won't if she hangs onto an idea of who she is. If the student stays with her present body, attends to the details of her experience, and unhesitatingly takes that experience on, she will inhabit dreamtime. Her memory and imagination will collaborate to draw not only from this lifetime, but from all lifetimes and even, from lifetimes before.

The Watcher and the Watched

10A. Follow the Leader, Calling Names
10B. Pebbles in the Pond
10C. Follow the Leader, Leader Emerging
10D. Pusher/Comeback
10E. Performance Score: Slow Motion Fight

Twenty students arrive between fifteen minutes to the hour and the hour. There's comraderie among them as they talk and exchange their street clothes for personalized tatters. One by one they walk onto the sprung-wood floor and find a place for themselves. Some lie down, some sit, some stand, and some move around the room. Bodies stretch and pull. Groans and moans. Pants, swooshes, gasps. Someone runs around mouthing raucous sounds. A soft, graceful hand floats along a wall. Someone tones, another writhes. However, they do it, each student finds a way to come into themselves, to come home.

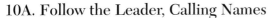

10A. Follow the Leader, Calling Names

• You'll play "Follow the Leader." When you hear me call your name, you know you're the Leader. The rest of the group will do whatever you do until I call the next name. (Of course, adjustments have to be made to accommodate physical limitations.) Do anything you want. Movement, vocalization, language, props, leave the room. Anything.

• Remember, this is the first exercise of the day. Do what you need to do to get here, into this room, into your body, to connect with your spirit and with one another.

• Leaders, see your actions within the context of the previous actions. Build off one another. When you hear your name called, continue on as Leader, right from where you are, from your action and from within your feeling. Don't feel pressured to entertain the group, or keep everybody busy.

• In a sense, there's a collaborative relationship between all the Leaders. You're building this event together. Towards the end, particularly the last person, take the group to closure.

F ollow the Leader calls forth the present-mindedness that is a basic component of improvisation. At the same time that you experience the seductive pleasures of being part of the pack, following the team, aimlessly, irresponsibly, your number may come up. You may be called on to lead. You can't leave yourself elsewhere, trodden under the heels of everyone else. You have to summon your power to lead from where you are, right there, right then and act on it.

> *"What do I do if I don't like what the Leader is doing? If I don't have that kind of energy, or physical capability? I personally object to that kind of content?"*

You try everything out whether you like it or not. Believing you can't be a certain way, or do a particular thing ("I'm this, I'm not that"), indicates that you think you already know that experience. In moment-to-moment awareness, that's never true. It's impossible to project into experience. Moments of experience are in reality different, the result of many influences. It's our minds which have a static idea of that experience. If we limit our mind, it will be limited.

All experience is in everyone of us. What we most detest in ourselves we will find in others. Once we move into the experience, we will see that it can be different if we allow it to *be*, that it is different by its own nature.

> *"But suppose the Leader is doing activity with no feeling, meaning or content? That doesn't inspire me and I feel uncomfortable with?"*

Our expectations control our experience, creating standards by which we judge everything. "That's right." "That's wrong." "That makes me happy." "That makes me feel pain." The problem with this is the "that makes me . . ." part. Our inner peace is determined by this self-created external fiction. Suppose we don't expect anything. Suppose we accept whatever we're presented with. The curiosity we respond with leads to not only acceptance, but, fascination with diversity.

This doesn't imply that we will become passive voyeurs "oohing" and "aahing" at unkind, or unjust, acts. Our responses to these occasions will be immediate and appropriate, unleashed from past ideology. Instead of emotionally motivated, they'll be compassionately charged.

Endings

Follow the Leader also gives practice in laying down stones. Each Leader adds a piece of the path. When John hears his name called, he begins to lay down the next segment as his part within the whole. How he's experienced the whole so far inspires his contribution.

The last person closes the event, preferably without feeling responsible for a "good ending." If she remains present and attentive to the unfolding experience, an ending will surface. A "good ending" will dictate the narrow demand, "Now I must make something interesting." This will usually be predictable and obvious; i.e., the flower folding its petals, or everyone laying down on the floor either in death or sleep, a group hug, exiting off the floor with an attitude that the exercise is over. When we finish this way we really don't end, we just vacate our experience.

Endings can surprise the "ender" and everyone involved. By staying present, with the trust that at some point an ending will appear, an ending *will* appear.

We're following a "big" mind that never ends and never closes. We're not making linear theater, with a beginning, middle and end. We're not looking for resolution. We may never resolve anything. But we recognize moments, when the idea, image or rhythmic pattern that we're engaged in can conclude. These cue moments that we can walk away from, that feel free, that we don't want any more or any less from. Our concept of endings becomes more and more unpredictable as we expand our awareness.

So far, the students have not had to pay attention to the collective rhythms. The Leader does something. Others copy it, simultaneously. Now, we graze away from the **Follow the Leader** sequence to an exercise that leads to "choice-ier" copying.

10B. Pebbles in the Pond

• Let's stand in a circle equidistant from each other. Each of us holds an imaginary bucket filled with pebbles. We're standing around a pond.

• In sequence, each of us will take a pebble, drop it into the pond and say the word "plunk." We may make short spaces between each other, sometimes, long spaces, sometimes, no spaces. Listen to the "plunks" and spaces that come before you and design your "plunk" and space responsively. We'll go around the circle a few times. Remember, we're not playing with how we say "plunk" but only with *when* we say "plunk." We want to focus particularly on the space between each "plunk."

• Second phase: anybody can "plunk" at any time. Listen to the spaces in between.

• Third phase: Again, anybody can "plunk" at any time. However, now, we're noticing patterns as they arise and then following them. Suppose we hear this sequence: "plunk, ... plunk, plunk." If we repeat it again, "plunk, ... plunk, plunk" and even a third time or more, we establish a pattern. The pattern will suggest its own transformation, or shift.

⌣ •

Pebbles in the Pond is another convention. When we say, " Pebbles in the Pond" we mean that our timing will be irregular. We'll live in the space between the fill as well as the fill between the space.

Patterns

Pebbles in the Pond is a practice of experiencing context. We listen to what surrounds our action. As our tuning skills become more precise, we notice that relationships occasionally repeat, forming a pattern. A pattern is a repeating configuration of elements, in this case "plunks."

Sometimes, we may want to create a pattern, set up a repeatable sequence and stay with it for some time. In a sense, the pattern limits exploration. But, it provides a boundary for spontaneous ranging, too. It creates a context for the improvisational approach: "These are the limitations. Let's follow the moments within them." Jazz musicians might do this with a single melody. A painter, with only straight lines. A poet, with the same few words. In this training, we do it with elements of expression. And here we're doing it with a blip of voice. "Plunk."

The pattern, itself, will tell us how to move out of it, whether to shift abruptly to something else, or transform gradually to other sequencing. All we have to do is listen. We can't go wrong.

We hear silence. If we define sound as that which stimulates our auditory nerves by vibrations, then silence also contains sound. We can hear the vibrations and they becomes part of our rhythms. As we stand in the circle, we value the rich vibrations we hear with "plunk" and the quality of sound we hear with no "plunk" equally.

⌣ •

10C. Follow the Leader, Leader Emerging

• Begin by standing in neutral. Again, play Follow the Leader. I won't call out names. Whenever you want, become Leader by "shifting," doing some-

thing very different than what's going on. Different physicality, different psychology, different spirit. Your shift is a response to the situation you've interrupted.

    Aidan leads, running to the wall, slamming against it, over and over again
    Bob interrupts, falling down to the floor, singing joyously
    Linda takes the lead by crawling over to another person, whispering numbers incessantly
    Guillermo leaps up and then squats, as a warrior

Francis draws her finger over her face and neck, making deep indents into her flesh

Uta spins around the room wailing

James asks people if they've seen anyone go by

John acts as though he wants to move but can't, as if he's paralyzed

Everyone "shifts," in response to the action they are in. They take the lead by providing the next step in the ongoing improvisation, the laying down of stones. The rest of the class follows, each individual's action timed as "pebbles in the pond."

Touch

On the third day of the training, students were asked not to touch each other. Emphasis was placed on autonomy and independence. Even when in relationship, students were requested to maintain physical, and, psychic separation.

Now, two weeks later, students are better prepared for physical contact. Their actions are guided by intention, and are physical expressions of internal experience. Every act carries meaning, and is a little window into their psyche. They know it.

10D. Pusher/Comeback

• In pairs. One of you is the Pusher. The other is the Comeback. Pusher, with your hands, apply force to different locations on the body of the Comeback. Vary the amount of force from feather light to the maximum power you think your partner can receive.

• Comeback, stand in an aligned posture, relaxed. Drop down into the ankle, knee and thigh joints as if you are somewhat sitting. This posture allows for a free and immediate response. Move with the pushes as you get them. Respond with the same amount of energy that you receive. The part of you that receives the contact is the first part to respond. The rest of your body follows through. For instance, if you get pushed on the back of the left shoulder, the back of your left shoulder is the first thing to move. If the touch is light enough, it may be the only thing to move. If the contact has more force to it, then the whole body accommodates the response. Whatever amount of force you move with, use it to bring you back to your original stable and relaxed posture. From there, you are ready to receive your next contact. If the contacts are coming fast and furiously, and they certainly may, always use whatever energy you are given to come back to a loose, neutral stance.

• There is a flow of energy between the Pusher and the Comeback. The Pusher initiates and the Comeback plays it out. One stream of energy.

• The Comeback uses only the momentum that is given, no more or no less. Don't resist. Don't anticipate. If the Pusher feels the Comeback's resistance, or anticipation, they let them know: "I feel that you're resisting," or, "I feel that you're anticipating."

• Both of you will have a turn playing out each role. After each of you have had a turn, we do another set. This time the Pusher uses different parts of her body to make the contacts. No hands.

• In the third and last set of this sequence, contacts are made with feeling. Tender, affectionate caresses, playful pokes, aggressive shoves. The Comeback "realizes" contacts as a series of "shifts," each one following on the previous one, in an unpredictable, yet cohesive, manner.

Another covenant comes into play here. Students agree that regardless of how they address one another during these exercises, it's not personal. They offer themselves as targets for the other's expressive practice. Everyone knows that everyone is practicing *on* everyone.

This exercise addresses physical and psychic skills. Alignment and balance result in responsive and graceful movement. A hard push can result in a face to the floor or a series of graceful turns, depending on the relaxed control of the Comeback. The body moves as a unit, beginning with the area of impact. As a dropped pebble creates consecutive ripples on the surface of a pond, so the movement gradually builds and, then, diminishes as it travels through the body. Eventually, the body returns to stillness. By trial and error, the Comeback discovers how to maintain a graceful balance while receiving any amount of energy the Pusher sends her way.

In many of the previous exercises, students have the opportunity to examine emotions as they arise. The roles of Pusher and Comeback are particularly loaded and offer, yet, another go at it. Since the action involves touch, all kinds of touch, it may invoke sensuality, anger, terror, hurtfulness, victimization, desire, aggression, and playfulness. Hopefully, these emotions won't overwhelm the players and inhibit their movement. It can happen, though. This is where the hardest lessons lie: energy is simply energy, empty of meaning. With the touch, images and memories may trigger and accompanying emotions surface. These can be noticed. But the students should move on and not become absorbed in these images. They are encouraged to remain focused on the energetic experience.

Pusher/Comeback is a collaboration. Energy is passed from one to another, each player creating one half of the choreography. Each response, whether thought, feeling, emotion or image, is grist for the mill

of awareness; to be looked at, breathed through, and played with. They fill physical shapes and actions with liveliness.

10E. Performance Score: Slow Motion Fight

• Let's form an audience. Two people go out onto the floor and face off. A third goes out to be the referee.

• The two perform a slow motion fight. Slow motion must be maintained so that no one gets hurt. The referee makes sure that the combatants remain extremely slow at all times.

• You both must respond to the contact you get from each other. You are pretending that you are the most vicious of enemies. When you get hit, your face and body shows that it really hurts. If you land a punch or a kick, you're overjoyed. Use that responsive energy to come back to your partner with another.

• Remember, the two of you are partners. You're collaborating on this fierce dance.

• The audience cheers and heckles, encouraging the combatants to fully allow feelings, expressions and actions of aggression to surface.

Slow motion stretches out time and everything within it. Each particle of feeling and action can be illuminated. This slowly, students can clearly track their process. Feelings such as rage, fear, hurt, and joy rise and fall, large waves coming in from the distance, overtaking the "fighter," and then subsiding. Whether or not the student is willing to ride these waves becomes evident.

Kai moves slowly until right before he lands a blow, then he speeds up to make his mark.

Carol strikes with her fingers rather than fist, her arm mov-

ing from her shoulder rather than her torso.

Hugh falls down and then lays there. Phil hangs back, waiting, for him to get up.

Susan and Michael can't play. They're laughing too hard.

Kai, Carol, Hugh, Phil, Susan and Michael are stuck in ideas about what they're doing and what it means. Kai really wants to win. Carol doesn't think she's the kind of person who hurts people. Neither does Hugh. Phil feels sorry for Hugh and politely waits for Hugh to take his turn. Susan thinks the whole thing is ridiculous and Michael doesn't think he should get fierce if she doesn't.

If these folks divorced themselves from personal identification with their selves, from a habitual way of looking at the particular form, "Fight," they'd be free to observe its elements. They could play "Fight" and notice how it *works:* the movements, facial expressions, timing between partners, rise and fall of feelings, and relationship to the audience. Glued to personal identification, they aren't free from their judgments and are dominated by the idea that the actions convey something about themselves personally. In order to truly enjoy this exercise, they need to see, that in terms of energy and form, there's no difference between hitting someone and being hit. Oppressor and oppressed are concepts we bring to activity. If students let go of these concepts, they can see a dance of movement and feeling. Energy is being exchanged.

If students are studying to be professional actors or performers, they might be called upon to play act a fight at some time in their career. They must be able to call up the feelings drawn upon in this exercise. But suppose students are not interested in performing. What's the value of this particular practice in a person's daily life?

Hidden Emotions

As long as we leave emotions unexplored, hidden below the threshold of our awareness, they remain encapsulated within fear. What we don't know, we're afraid of. We create judgments and opinions about these emotions to keep them at bay. We consider others who exhibit them as different than ourselves. We're foreigners in our own bodies.

The Action Theater training never asks for particular emotions. Students are never asked to be anything—happy, sad, or angry. Instead, structures, such as this one, awaken emotions. A fight will certainly stimulate particular emotions.

All emotions are in all of us. For some, if these emotions are never owned, explored, or played with, they erupt in devious ways, unconsciously and maybe even destructively. If one tours one's own inner landscape with awareness, inhabiting all experiences as they arise, then one discovers that what was feared is not fearful. A fully embodied experience is quite different from the projected experience.

Emotions are not "things" in themselves. They can never be known or presumed. They don't themselves carry inherent threat. They are configurations of our energy brought on by a certain environment. This environment may be the state of our mind and body at the time, the dynamics between me and another, my surroundings, whether I'm alone or not. Emotions never occur the exact same way. They're only what we make of them. We create their substance and characteristics. We are not them, nor they us.

In **Slow Motion Fight,** we're fighting friends. We feel rage. It's obviously not at my friend. Therefore, I must be relating to something within me, my rage. These others are collaborators in my drama. If I only dance my own stories, I'll never open up to any truly spontaneous possibilities.

Response

11A. Polarities
11B. Fast Track
    1. Sound and Movement Mirror
    2. Sound and Movement Responses
11C. "It" Responds
11D. Performance Score: Back to Front

Black and white. Heavy and light. Hot and cold. Elements we think of as opposites need each other to exist. They rest on each other and are of each other. For instance, hot has coldness in it. Otherwise, we wouldn't call it hot. Coldness is missing hot. Therefore, cold. The same with dark and light. Light is less dark. And dark is more of what used to be light.

Or, we could look at it this way. Hot is not hot at all, and has nothing to do with cold. It's a configuration of sensations which occur only when I experience them. So, hot, now, is not the hot of later nor before. This hot is never to be repeated the same way again. Its context will always be different. But, we repeat the words "hot" and "cold" depending on them to be identical.

11A. Polarities

• Everyone, find a place for yourself on the floor and stand. Turn your attention to your breath. With each out-breath, let go of any tension that you don't need in order to stand.

• I'm going to call out pairs of words, and I would like you to explore movement that these words suggest.

In, out.
Up, down.
Slow, fast.
Hard, soft.
Curve, straight.
Heavy, light.
Push, pull.
Fixed location, travel.
Open, close.
Tense, relax.

• As I direct you through these opposites, I'm going to side-coach you; I'll be talking to you from the side-lines. You don't have to look at me, nor do you have to stop what you're doing. Just let my words in as you concentrate on what you're doing.

• Keep your timing irregular. As your body passes through different shapes, or forms, you may imagine, or notice, different states of minds connected to them. Let these states of mind surface. Allow them to affect what you're doing, the tension in your body, the expression on your face, the focus of your eyes. Let your energy be spontaneous, fickle, and erratic. If you feel confused, scared, in an unknown place, be conscious of your choice to either move further towards that feeling, or veer away from it. Enjoy yourself.

• In the next few moments, relate to someone near you. Continue moving through these qualities, randomly (at your choice) in relation to one another. Both of you may or may not be playing with the same quality. Sometimes, you may want to relate within similar energy and, sometimes, you may want to contrast with each other. Respond to your inner impulses while you also respond to the actions of your partner.

Movement is a treasure to be enjoyed. We may carry thoughts and feelings about our bodies, or bodies in general, that prevent us from experiencing movement pleasurably. So occasionally, we need to approach this pleasure through the back door. An exercise such as **Polarities** turns the student's interest toward investigation. Their attention will be on the concept of opposites, and they use their bodies as clues in an scavenger hunt, seeing what they can come up with. Hopefully, pleasure will sneak up on them while they're looking in another direction.

For a student unaccustomed to this kind of physical exploration, it is very tempting to focus on the intellectual concept of "up," for instance, verses "down." Finding movement only from inside the "How can I think about up?" procedure is tremendously limited. Thoughts can only come from what they already know—from old thoughts—and those old thoughts usually produce realistic, or imitative, action. On the other hand, sensing "up" movement kinetically, rather than thinking out a solution, then playing within the parameters of sensation, will guide the student into undefined, untested and unchartered surprise.

We inhabit our bodies as idiosyncratically as who we are. Some of us *think* our way in. We consider way too much, freeze up, atrophy. We think we may break if we shake things up. So, we don't shake at all. We don't even sway. Others of us throw movement away as if it's trash and we don't want it. We're wild, raw and even appear free. We might even mistake our spinning maelstrom of energy and activity as freedom. Actually, we're moving too fast to feel anything.

Consider this: your body is a chisel, the space around you is stone. Your movements carve into the stone. Each gesture, each bit of action and shape, scribes a mark into an undisturbed and dense surface. Not one iota of movement can occur without leaving its signature. Even the blink of your eye makes an inscription on the stone of space. How would this change your relationship toward your physical actions? How would you pay attention?

Here comes a fast drill. Quick shifts. No time to think.

11B. Fast Track

1. Sound and Movement Mirror

• Everyone, stand in two lines, facing each other with about 8 feet between you. One line will be the Leaders and the other will be the Followers. The first two people in each line, run toward each other. When they reach the center, the Leader does a short sound and movement action. The Follower mirrors it immediately, almost simultaneously. When they're finished, they run back to their places in line while the next two people run forward toward each other. This repeats until every couple in the line has had a turn. Then the progression comes back up the line.

• Switch roles and repeat this sequence. Remember that the leading and the following happen simultaneously.

Dialogue:
"I need time to get what my partner's doing."
"What do you do in that time?"
"I try to understand."
"What are you doing to understand?"
"I'm thinking about what the action means."
"Don't understand, do!"

We don't think feeling. Feeling doesn't come into us that way and it doesn't come into us from the outside either. We don't need to understand another's feeling in order to empathize with them. Knowing another's feelings happens without mental interference. We know by intuition. We can feel what the other feels because we *know* all feelings. Feelings are in us already. We only need to intend to feel what the other feels.

In this case, the Follower either "gets it," or doesn't "get it," and that's irrelevant anyway. There's nothing to understand. There's only something to copy.

Often, doing triggers being. When students "put on" their partner's action, they may experience the being of it just by relaxing, by allowing the action to overtake them. The action, then, does them.

2. Sound and Movement Response

• Here, the basic structure remains the same: Two people run toward each other. This time however, one does a sound and movement action and freezes in the final shape of that action. The other person performs a response that's different in form and content. You're no longer mirroring. As they return to their place in line, the next pair runs forward, the Leader initiating a new sound and movement.

Dialogue
"If I don't understand the meaning of the act, what am I responding to?"

"What are you doing when you respond?"

"I'm trying to figure out what I see coming from my partner and then I'm thinking about how I should respond appropriately."

"There's no time for that. The action and the response happen immediately in sequence, on one release of energy: both actions, sequentially, ride the same wave."

A and B run in.

A does an action.

B sees that action and allows herself to feel it.

B responds to what she feels by doing a different action.

For a moment, B lets A in. B receives A's feelings, state of mind, energy no matter what it is. B takes it on, sensing what that particular state is like, energetically, kinetically and in feeling. B now "knows" A's action as a bodily experience and responds impulsively, reflexively. No thought. No time. No understanding. No "B," in a sense. The response does itself. The more open B's imagination, the more territory is available for responding.

◖ •

11C. "It" Responds

Divide into groups of four. This is similar to the Empty Vessel exercise. One person singled out is approached by each of the others in turn with a condition, and possibly a situation, using movement, sound or language. Instead of mirroring that situation as in Empty Vessel, the "It" person responds to the approacher with a contrasting form. If they approach with movement, then you can only use sound and language. If they use language and movement, then you can only use sound. In other words, the approacher provides one half of a scene and the "It" person provides the other half. Both the approacher and the "It" person interact within their forms until a new approacher interrupts. The three approachers work quickly, reading each scene as it develops and then interrupting with an immediate response. Approachers, don't be too literal or realistic.

◖ •

Primary/Secondary Shifts

A **primary shift** initiates a scene change, whether it be a situation, change in environment, psychological or physical action. A **secondary shift** directly responds to the **primary shift**. Primary shifts initiate change; secondary shifts accommodate. In this exercise, the primary shifters are the approachers; they introduce new information. "It" is the secondary shifter. Each approacher offers the responder a primary shift. The responder ("It" person) replies with a secondary shift.

Direct/Indirect Relationship

A response may either be direct or indirect. A **direct** response enters into the same time and space as the initial action. The performers acknowledge one another and inhabit the same world. For example, a performer curls into a ball on the floor and cries, "I'm wax. I'm melting." In direct response, a partner might respond by standing above them, waving a hand, gleefully hissing, "See my flames. They will burn you." If that same performer responded by standing bolt upright, saying, " Last night I dreamt I was being attacked," or ran around the room waving their arms and crying, or squatted behind the person while rubbing their hands together and chanting a lyrical melody, her responses would be indirect. **Indirect responses** do not share the same space and time as the initial action. The performers do not acknowledge one another nor do they inhabit the same world. An indirect response adds different worlds to the scene.

Situation/Condition

What's the difference between a situation and a condition?

To make things easy, let's say that a **situation** refers to external happenings, locations, events, relationships, environments. **Condition** refers to internal feelings, mind states, physical handicaps, styles or peculiarities, possessions—as in being possessed. Situations come and go but conditions are always in us. We're always someplace internally. Even if that place feels like "no place," then "no place" is the place, the condition we're in.

For example:

Conditions: a stiff leg, a heavy energy, intoxicated, spastic, darting eyes, calm, introverted, exhausted, afraid, unable to speak, hysterical, hungry, etc.

Situations: Being introduced, coming home, on a train, a surgeon operating, falling from a cliff, in bed, walking through India, turning a corner, etc.

Both the primary shifter and the secondary shifter always communicate condition. They may or may not communicate situation.

Susan approaches Juan. She's tossing imaginary somethings around her onto the ground as if she is feeding birds. At the same time, she looks afraid and her actions are abrupt, angular, tense. After noticing her fear, Juan responds by pretending to lurk behind a tree while whispering to her about a debt owed to him by his closest friend. His manner is outwardly calm and soothing, but inwardly foreboding. He acknowledges her fear while adding an entirely new element (the situational business about the debt) into the scene.

Both Susan and Juan are communicating condition and situation: they also respond to each other's condition and situation. Had Susan only expressed her condition (fear, agitation) and stood relatively still on the stage, no situation would have been indicated. Juan could have offered a situation to give Susan's action a context, e.g., he could have talked as he did, but on a telephone indicating a past or future interaction between them. Time, space and ordering of events are always open to the imagination in this process.

Contrasting Forms

Why contrasting forms?

By insisting that the form of the response be different than the stimulus, the responder is forced to *see*. They must notice the shape of the action, how it moves in space, the quality of its sound or language, and its rhythm. They look, listen and feel. Their response, then, comes from an embodied experience. Since they can't fall into the same form as the initiator (which is always very tempting), they must search for a different response. Even if their response is logical and simple, they must change their perspective and expand its representation.

This requirement may plunge the student into an analytical mode, dictating to themselves, analyzing everything they notice, checking and rechecking to make sure they noticed what they think they noticed, and then, weighing all the possibilities for response. With practice, the choice of contrasting forms becomes second nature and becomes the most enticing stroke to make.

We're not looking for realistic scenes, scenes that copy "real" life, as television does, or the movies. We strive for more unchartered waters, as we put images and actions side by side that don't normally come packaged that way. Our scenes are like dreams: the chain of events, though stimulated by each other, come from realms of the psyche that aren't necessarily ordered by usual time and space. The logic that connects the images is as fresh and uncanny as the individuals' imagination allows.

11D. Performance Score: Back to Front

• Five people: go out on the floor and stand side by side with your backs toward us. The rest of us are an audience. In random sequence, each of you turn to face the audience. Begin a monologue and continue with it until you get interrupted. As soon as you get interrupted, turn back around.

• Have all the monologues contrast with one another. Each time you begin a monologue, it should be very different from the other ones you have heard and the ones you have started—different in the content of the language, the timing and quality of the voice, different energy. Interrupt each other erratically. You are playing together, the interruptions, timing, and quality of your voices are all part of a musical event. Don't bridge content—each other's words, or style of voice—in any way. After five minutes or so, all of you face front, talk simultaneously and orchestrate your voices until you find an ending.

This score is about music and dancing. The five partners dance together with their voices and their back-to-front turns. The interruptions, pauses, accelerations, highs and lows, fasts and slows, crescendos and retards, are manifestations of energy translated into sound. The energy flows out of, and into, itself. The participants release into that flow. The content serves the flow, too. Listening arouses feeling, feeling elicits image, and then, collectively, listening, feeling and image choose the sound quality.

When you think too much, you can't hear anything other than your thinking. You can't hear the music that's outside of your head, which is there all the time. Don't think. Just listen. Then, let the spaces be filled when you hear the need. Fill the spaces with a voice that pleases you, and content that arrives when you open the doors of silence.

For example:

Juanita is listening. The last two voices have been light, sing-song; one describing a journey in the desert and the other looking in the mirror at its nakedness. She interrupts with a loud, commanding monologue of instructions for assembling an outdoor barbeque. After only a few words, Joe interrupts with a return to the soft sing-song texture recounting an accident at summer camp. Shortly, Phil interrupts with, again, a harsh and abrupt style describing an encounter with a malfunctioning parking meter. Juanita interrupts with a sweet, silly description of a gladiola as it blooms. Phil interrupts with a sneering laugh describing a threatening prison experience.

Each of the situations described above could have been delivered with different voices, attitudes, coloring, timing and texture. But because of what the participants heard they chose the feelings and voices to follow the music, playing with similarity, contrast, rapid interruptions, sometimes settling into longer monologues. The content served the music and the music served the content.

Students are encouraged to develop content that means something to them, stimulates feeling, and resonates with their being. In **Back to Front,** they're listening and jumping into holes. They don't know what they're jumping in with exactly. They don't know what they're going to say, or how long they get to say it. A sound, or a short word, is enough. A "So," or "They," or "Do." As they listen to themselves, they build their text, voice, image and feeling, word by word.

Usually, when we interact with others through language, we listen for the conceptual and psychological content. Here, as in earlier exercises, we're listening to the pure sounds as well, the sounds devoid of meaning.

The interruptions are an integral part of the collective music. There's no question of competition, or control. When interrupted, whatever material is being pursued immediately gets dropped. No attachments to story, emotion, or completion. The intent is on listening and music making.

Action is, in fact, a response.
      That's all.

To act is to respond to the material of one's awareness: information from the senses, imagination, memory.

To act is to enact the current experience of awareness as it awares.

Day Twelve

A Scene

12A. 30 Minutes, Eyes Closed

12B. Non-Stop Talk /Walk

12C. Talking Circle

    1. One Word

    2. Two Words

    3. Few Words and Gesture

12D. Contenting Around

12E. Performance Score: Scene Travels

Our Vocabulary:

Sensation: What we see, hear, smell, taste, touch and kinetically experience.

Feeling: States of mind and body that can't be named but are familiar.

Thought: Analytical, judgmental, conceptual, reasoning, reflective, or planning mental activity.

Emotion: Thought inspired, identifiable states of mind.

Memory: Images, thoughts, feelings retained from past "real" life experience.

Imagination: The forming of mental or physical images of what is not present. Creating new images from the combination of any of the above.

Action: Behavior.

Experience arises from the interaction of any or all of the above. Sensation, feeling, thought, memory, imagination and action. As long

as we continue to notice information coming in and from within, without lingering, without preference to outcome, we call our experience, "Present."

Every week we close our eyes, each week for a longer period. The experience is always different, for we feel safer and safer in the darkness. Each time we are more comfortable with ourselves from the inside.

12A. 30 Minutes Eyes Closed

• Everybody find a place for yourself on the floor and either stand, sit, or lie down. Get comfortable and close your eyes. Bring your attention inside yourself. Relax. Focus on your breath. Notice how the air comes in and goes out. Notice the sensations that surround that experience. Every time your breath goes out, relax your body and your mind even more. Let go of the tension that forms thoughts.

• Keep your eyes closed for the next thirty minutes. Shortly after I stop talking, begin to move. Notice a sensation in your body and move into it. Or just start moving. Whatever happens happens. Follow your movement. Listen to it. Listen to it from the inside of it. Allow what you hear to cue you, lead you. There's nothing to understand, like or dislike. You're noticing designs the course. You don't have to create anything. You are responding to what you notice. . . . Whatever you're doing right now, intensify it. Go further into it. Give over to it. If you're moving into a very soft, "void-y" kind of place, go further into that void. If you're moving into a hard, tense place, go further into that. If you're moving into a painful place, go further into the pain. If you're moving into fun and play, be even more playful. Keep from naming, labeling, talking or reporting to yourself. Continue to notice sensation. Continue to notice feeling. Whatever you notice. Sweat, hard breath, calm, still, whatever. . . . If you come in physical contact with another body in the room, do whatever you want. Play, mess around, get hard, get soft. Do whatever you want. Follow sensation and feeling. If you want to withdraw, leave it, then leave it. Whatever you want is perfect.

As soon as the eyes close the pressure's off. There's no where and no thing to go to, make, do, or be. I'm only with myself, here, laying on the floor. My observing mind notices sensation in my shoulder, the weight of it, how it presses on the floor. I press more and feel the bone, the hardness, the mass. Bump, bang, slide the bones, more bones, dry bones, brittle, breakable, dig in and in and in. Tunneling in and in, deep into dark matter, thick surroundings, mouth opening, pulling back into neck, back arched, opening the belly, stretching, bursting. . . .

Eyes Closed is a physical exercise. We let the body lead. Feeling, memory, imagination and thought respond to the sensations of the body. Action results. That action is experienced as sensation. A feedback loop between sensation, feeling, memory, thought, imagination, and action develops. One ignites another. In any order. At any time.

Sometimes an image, thought or feeling pulls attention from sensation. You may be moving an arm, then suddenly believe you're moving your arm towards something, and discover that while you were thinking that plan, you've forgotten how it felt to get there, you only got there. Stay present. Throughout **Eyes Closed**, students are reminded to return to sensation.

"Whatever you're doing now, go further."

What does that mean? Faster, bigger, louder or more tense? Maybe. Or, maybe it means that whatever you are noticing at the moment, you accept and explore with undisturbable devotion. Maybe you're already on your way, rising and falling into realms of unexplored behavior. Maybe you just need a nudge, a prod to remind you that you can let the reins out.

Going Inside

A student may come upon an emotional block. The feeling could be overwhelming. Tears spill. The student gets caught in emotion. What triggered the emotion may be somewhere underneath the threshold of awareness, from a remembered, or imagined, thought or image. To return to the present, she must return to the immediate experience. Go inside of it. Investigate its sound, energy, texture. Discover its legs, head, hands.

When we go *inside* of crying, we become foreigners to it. We're no longer in the familiar of crying. Think of it. When we cry, our attention fixes on a painful idea, or thought. If instead, we let go of the thought and change our focus to the crying itself, to the actual experience of crying, we become a landscape of sound, energy, movement, weight. We're present.

12A. Eyes Closed, Continuing

• Be still exactly where you are. Don't move. Anything. . . . Take your time and open you eyes. . . . Don't move anything else. . . . Now slowly, very slowly, come to standing and begin a very slow walk in the room. . . . As you walk, bring your attention back into this room. Notice the others. . . . Pick up speed, go little faster. Feel each other. Look at each other. Be here.

Again, as in Day Five, we move fairly rapidly from inner focus to outer. No lingering. Nothing terribly important one place or the other.

Let's talk.

12B. Nonstop Talk/Walk

• Walk. As you're walking, avoid circling. Change your direction arbitrarily every once in a while. I'd like you to be talking constantly, a non-stop stream of consciousness babble. Let one idea take you to your next idea. Listen to yourself. Listen to what you are saying. . . .

• When you pass somebody in the room, and you hear a few words, or a few phrases out of context, shift your text to accommodate the material that you just heard, and either bring that material into your text, or start a new text, by shifting and beginning new material off of what you just heard.

• Begin to spend some time silently walking and occasionally pause, stand still. Listen to the other voices. Then, relate your walking, the where and when of it, to your talking. Have all of your choices respond to what you're hearing, seeing, feeling, and imagining. Stay with your own content. Avoid blending, responding or using the same language.

• Now, you're working as an ensemble.

This is an exercise in non-functional languaging. Or, at least, non-functional in the way we're used to thinking about language. Here, we're not talking to anybody. We're not talking in order to get anything to happen, change anything, or make an effect. We're just talking to talk. To feel the whole feel of talk.

Students enter this with varying degrees of self-consciousness. For example: "I really don't have anything to say, so I'll just repeat myself for a while," or "I'll report some current events that have happened to me lately," or "I'll describe the room," or "How I'm feeling right now, or what the others are wearing," or "I'll comment on *what* the others are saying," and so on. All of these tactics place the emphasis on what is being *said* rather than the *saying*. The experience of talking slips by unnoticed because we get caught in content. The content, or thought, that resulted in the crying example described earlier, blinded the student to the action of crying. The student has prejudged the exercise as difficult and is trying to cope with the problem.

Again and again, students are encouraged to listen to themselves, to really hear not only the content but the structure of what they're saying in detail: the words, parts of words, sounds of their voices, rhythms, the feel of their mouths as it forms language, their chests as they breathe out the words. And to give themselves time. Often they need to slow down, so the imagination can interrupt the habitual, so the onslaught of words and ideas that only recount life can become life.

When the student gives up control, the language languages them, as does the language of the other students. Once they experience language as separate from themselves, something they can dance with and aren't bound to, they hear all language in the same way. Incorporation of others' texts, or shifting their own text in association to what they hear, comes easy; no energy is wasted on a particular outcome, ending, story, logic or reason.

12C. Talking Circle

1. One Word

• Everyone, come stand in a tight little circle, shoulder to shoulder. We're going to play an association game. One of you says a word and the next person will say a word in response. We'll continue around the circle with each person saying a word in response to the word that has just been said. Move quickly around the circle, no time to think, stay in the present, listening and responding. As much as you can, stay relaxed. Breathe. Stay focused on what you're doing. If you find yourself starting to laugh, or fidget, notice how that's keeping you from fully engaging in the process.

2. Two Words

• Let's change the direction. We're going to go around the circle the opposite way, and this time, everyone says two words. Keep it moving, so there is no time between the words.

3. Few Words and Gesture

• Change the direction again. Now, speak a few words and add a simple gesture as you speak. Choose a gesture that is in some way relevant to the words you are saying.

• Let's sit down and tell a story together. Each person will add one word. Listen to the tone, pitch, and rhythm of the words as they are said and allow this to affect the way you say your word.

• Again, sit in a circle. This time each of us will add a few words in order to build a narrative together. Our primary interest is to explore the possibilities of language as sound. Let go of the content and hear the sound of what is being said. Listen to the pitch, rhythm, volume, enunciation and articulation of the words. Play with these when you're the speaker.

We hear differently. Some of us, upon hearing a word, experience a feeling. Some see an image in our mind's eye. Others hear the sound of the word, particularly the music and rhythm. And there are those who experience the word kinesthetically. Of course, if we're distracted while the word is being spoken, then none of these processes happen. There's no room. If we're trying to figure out our response even before we hear the word, we receive the word only as an idea. When there is direct and unmitigated listening, the response, the association, arrives. It's as if its already there. The next link on a chain.

Phrase and Gesture

The physical gesture that accompanies each phrase may be approached in several ways. The most logical way would be for the gesture to (1) literally depict the meaning of the phrase. Additionally, it may (2) reflect the subtext feeling or mind state. The gesture might just as easily (3) indicate a story element that would elaborate the phrase. Or (4) it may reflect something far fetched and be arrived at by association.

Phrase	Gesture
1. "sun shines"	arms circle over head and quiver
2. "sun shines"	face smiles, relaxes, smiles, relaxes
3. "sun shines"	rapid desperate digging at the ground in desperation
	or
	walks as if parched and weak
	or
	grabs and rips at head
4. "sun shines"	typing on typewriter

Now, we have some tools. Our imagination is ignited. We're expressing images through language and movement. We're feeling connected. We're listening to each other. These are the building blocks toward scene making.

Scene Making

A scene is a series of events held together by some commonality. Often one event is seen in light of another. On the traditional stage, a scene is built around a psychological problem that surfaces between the characters. Then, it is addressed by either disclosure, investigation or resolution.

In our terms, a scene may be held together by a far greater range of concepts. A single image might carry a scene, or a rhythm, or a feeling. Within the parameters, an investigation proceeds. The investigation becomes the scene.

Since we improvise, how do we set these parameters? How do we create a cohesive scene?

Tree

The structure of a tree serves as a useful image or map. Different parts of the scene correspond to different parts of the tree. The central theme, from which all the other ideas stem, is the trunk. Background, or supporting material, corresponds to the roots. Larger themes, manifestations or implications, correspond to the branches. Tangential associations correspond to the leaves or fruit. Sometimes, these appear singly or in clusters. One of these associations may fall off the tree and introduce a new trunk: a nut dropping from the branches of the first tree. This takes root and begins another scene. Soon, there could be a whole grove, an entire forest of scenes that sprout from each other.

The following exercise is based on the tree. It deals with language. Later, we'll bring in action.

12D. Contenting Around

• Sit on the floor in trios and face one another. One of you begins a monologue. You are laying out the trunk. The next person has three choices: either repeat what was just said, add on to it continuing the same form and content, or shift to a new monologue, with different form and content, providing branches, roots, leaves, fruit or nuts. Take short turns. A few lines. If you shift, arrive at that shift by association. Remember the association comes from *present* experience. Not just an idea. You're filling out a single tree or planting a grove.

• Once this process begins, continue going round and round in sequence until I say stop. Then, begin another round with the next person starting the thing off. We'll do this three times so that you each can initiate a sequence.

⌣ •

The first person who speaks lays down the trunk. Everything that follows is developed in some relation out of it. The clearer the initial image, the more contained and cohesive the scene will be. A trunk usually has within it a larger idea, concept, image or feeling that has the potential to inspire subsidiary feelings and images.

Every trunk, branch, root, leaf, nut and fruit may be developed, filled out, and given body. As the participants go round and round, they may relate to anything that has come before them, drawing from their memory, feelings, and imagination.

The tree metaphor relates directly to laying down stones mentioned previously. In both models, the student walks backwards, seeing the item laid down before her, staying connected to the unfolding which, then, inspires her present action. Both attempt to organize what may be vastly overwhelming possibilities.

The structure of *tree* could include *laying down stones* but *laying down stones* doesn't necessarily presuppose *tree.* For in order to work with the *tree*, students must be able to listen and remember all that occurred in the scene *(laying down stones).* The difference between the two is that the *tree* leads to a cohesive scene, wherein every action and image share a common base. *Laying down stones* does not particularly lead to cohesiveness. The *stones* require only noticing and remembering what went before. The content, even though relational, may be a seemingly arbitrary string of associations.

In the exercise above, we're limiting ourselves to language. We can use the tree metaphor with movement or sound, too.

The following exercise brings movement, sound and language into the forest.

◡•

12E. Performance Score: Scene Travels

• Six or seven people stand at the far wall facing the audience. You're going to sound, language, and gesture a scene together. Your scene begins at the far wall and will end when you reach the front floor boards. You travel forward as a group.

• Imagine that, collectively, you are a giant organism. As each part of the organism moves forward, it extends out of the whole, but remains part of the whole. As you each travel forward, you either speak or sound. As you move forward, you're continually creating and re-creating a collective shape. You're building content either by repeating what has already been said, adding on to what has been said, or jumping off into a new direction that is relevant. More than one person can talk at a time if you're speaking roughly the same language and orchestrating your voices.

• Don't rush. Stay with sounds, phrases, counterpoints, mini-choruses as they arise. Join each other. You may interrupt each other. If you get interrupted, you must become silent and stop moving. If you're not travelling, hold your last shape, be silent and still. You all reach the front and finish more or less simultaneously.

◡•

As this event happens, students don't consciously work the tree. It would slow them down, interrupt the flow, and take them out of the scene. The tree is only useful as a model to help conceptualize a scene. What is the scene? How does it hang together? Once we get the idea of relatedness that the tree offers, we can forget the tree and just go about making scenes.

Every solution has a danger. Here, the danger is that the scenes may become too "worked." Everyone tries too hard to stay related. For example: the first person that leaves the wall may say something about birth. Thereafter, everyone clings to the concept of birth, and pretty soon, there's an assortment of clever and witty ideas about birth. Nothing new. No surprises.

Students must simultaneously experience and disengage from the unfolding content to give memory and imagination the room to pull the scene in unexpected directions. We don't listen only with our ears. Every cell is alert, sensing the collective heartbeat. Individuals unify, agree. Always. The event unfolds as a piece of music, as a movie moving.

Students relinquish their attachment to "I" and to "I's" ideas. They *are* feeling, thinking, remembering and imagining. They don't miss a beat. The music is continuous even when there's silence.

Action as Sign

13A. Pillows
13B. Image Making
13C. One Sound/One Move/One Speak
13D. Solo: Separate Sound, Movement and Language
13E. Trios: Separate Sound, Movement and Language
13F. Performance Score: Separate Sound, Movement and
　　　Language

*Three actors are on the stage. The play has begun. A woman stands
in a sliver of light on the edge of the stage, separated from the play.
Her job is to translate the text for the audience members who are
hearing-impaired. Her actions are simple, precise. She means them,
feels them, and for that moment, lives completely in the world from
which they spring. Her hands, eyes, eyebrows, lips are alive with
feeling. Musically, she depicts a symbology, a code, that is, to me,
undecipherable and, at the same time, understandable.*

　　*I shut my ears to the voices of the actors and only watch her
signs. Her actions are full of meaning and devoid of story.*

Signs

Our actions, speech, sounds, and gestures are signs that point to meaning. They represent concepts, images, feelings, information—something
different than what they are propelling, energy and vibrations through
space. Depending on how we open or tighten our perceptive lens, we
either see what's being represented or the representation itself. With
every word we say, there is the physical experience of making the sound,

what that physical experience evokes, the actual thing being talked about and what that evokes. Take the word "sister." I say, "Sister." I enunciate and intone "sister" this way or that. "Sister" is not the person, not the girl. It's a sign; a sound that comes out of my mouth. *How* I say "sister" gives some more signs about the concept of "sister," or something about me in relation to what "sister" means.

Sign language is set, prescribed, taught and learned. Our language is prescribed, taught and learned, but we learn ways to vary it. In order not to fall into clichéd language, we have to reinvent it as we go.

~ •

13A. Pillows

• Now, we'll do an ensemble event with Sounders and Movers. I've arranged some pillows in a corner, on the edge of the floor. That's the area for the Sounders. The empty floor is the area for the movers. If you're sitting on the pillows you're a Sounder and are collaborating on the sound score with everyone else on the pillows. If you're on the floor, you're a Mover.

• Switch back and forth between these positions at least three times during this twenty minute period. When you switch from Mover to Sounder and Sounder to Mover, do it with intention. Stay relevant to the scene.

• Sounders, you're working together as one voice, listening and following the sound as you hear it. You may all be playing with the same vocal pattern, or you may be in counterpoint, different patterns interacting with one another. You don't have to sound the movement that you see on the floor. Your job is to create a rich and varied sound space. And your job is to listen to the whole.

• Movers, begin moving solo for the first five minutes or so. Use this time to come into yourself, to connect with your body, sensations and feeling. Follow awareness. After about five minutes, begin to relate to the other people on the floor. Either join what they are doing or contrast it. Gradually open up to everybody on the floor. You are working as a collective, creating scenes together.

• Play with building tension between the Movers and the Sounders, so that if the sound is quiet and contained, your movement might be explosive, or if the sound dips and becomes dark, your movement might rise into lightness. Allow the sound to infect and inspire you, but not control you.

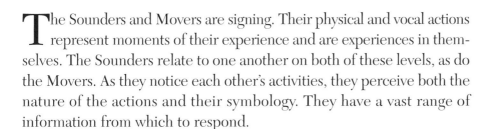

The Sounders and Movers are signing. Their physical and vocal actions represent moments of their experience and are experiences in themselves. The Sounders relate to one another on both of these levels, as do the Movers. As they notice each other's activities, they perceive both the nature of the actions and their symbology. They have a vast range of information from which to respond.

First Action

The first action, whether it be sound or movement, initiates the improvisation, and from then on, everything is part of the improvisation. There's no stepping out until the end. The improvisation contains all of the experience. If someone gets lost, or heady, thoughtful, etc., the improvisation contains all that, too. It contains everything that happens inside and outside of the mind. It's an extremely simple point, but a crucial one.

Always in the Scene

Students often forget that they're always part of the scene.

> *Joyelle is improvising. Sometimes she's engaged and committed to her actions, and other times she's on the sidelines, watching what others are doing, trying to figure it out, or contemplating her next move. In these moments, she feels lost, stuck or confused.*

Literally, she's lost her senses. She's not aware of herself, or of herself within the context of the improvisation. She's forgotten that she is. She's forgotten that she's always operating within a context, that the improvisation (life) is going on around her and she's in it whether she remembers it or not. Everything around her is still happening. Her partners on the stage see her in it. The audience sees her in it. Only Joyelle doesn't see herself in it.

If Joyelle remembered herself, remained in her body, her senses, she could then use her watching, planning, judging, and even her lost-ness, as material to embody, image, or role play. She could remain in the scene. It's a matter of her awareness.

In **Pillows**, even the role change from Sounder to Mover, or Mover to Sounder is within the improvisation. The role change move is relevant to the improvisation at that moment, since, even then, there is no way out.

━ •

13B. Image Making

• Let's stand in a circle. Each of us will describe an image in a few words, and we'll go around the circle.

• Now, we'll go around the circle again. We'll work with the same image, but this time express it a different way. In other words, change the way you use the language to get the picture, or experience, across.

• Now, we'll go around the circle one more time and, again use the same image, but change the form of the language, the words you choose, and the way you express and order them, still getting the initial image, or experience, across.

━ •

Example:

   *1st) A woman kneels beside the river and pounds her fists into
the water.*

   *2nd) Hit, slap, pound, smack. On my knees. The river listens.
On my knees. I hurt.*

   *3rd) She falls to her knees amid screams of horror, pounds the
water, the river rushes. Fists, fists. Ahhh, Ahhh, Ahhh, Ahhh.
Fists, fists, Ahhh, Ahhh, Ahhh.*

Pretend you're a poet. Mess around with the language. Move pieces ahead or forward. Enjoy the way the words sound. Like the rhythms. Experiment. Languaging is its own experience. It's a separate experience from what it represents. Different ordering of words, speaking of words, rhythms, pauses, and voices result in different experience. And vice versa.

   We describe, question, speak from inside experience, make lists, report, make sense, don't make sense, make commentary, analyze, reason, gossip, dialogue, monologue, count, repeat, puzzle, rhyme, abstract, concretize, pray....

   Make an image. Try each of the above. And even find more forms.

13C. One Move/One Sound/One Speak

• Everyone, arrange yourselves into trios. You'll build an improvisation together. Each of you will play different roles. One will be Mover, one Sounder and one Speaker. We will do three rounds, so that you will have a chance to explore each role.

• The Mover takes care of movement. The Sounder and Speaker must sound and speak without moving. Absolutely. No movement at all, except facial expression. The Sounder and Speaker may only move to change location and shape. It might not be appropriate for you to speak, or sound, from the posture that you are in; you may have to change posture and location to accommodate your intention. You may re-shape and relocate as often as you want. You are part of the whole picture, the image.

• Even though you're playing different roles, you're always in a time/space/ shape relationship with others and the room. Be aware of the whole picture and the whole sound, moment-to-moment. If you are, then every action will be relevant to the whole of everything.

• Each of you draws from your own internal landscape while responding to the images, sounds, and feelings presented by your partners.

• Speaker and Sounder, you are collaborating on the sound space, so listen to each other.

• Speaker, experience the sound of your language, the shape of your mouth, the feel of your tongue. Don't let the content of what you are saying overrule your experience.

• Mover, pay attention to detail, to the spatial relationship with the Sounder and Speaker. Acting out what you are hearing is, of course, one choice, but you may also draw from your imagination, make associations and then shape accordingly.

• Everyone, follow awareness.

• When I call stop, talk about what you liked and didn't like, how you might make it clearer, tighter, more connected, musical and, of course, lively.

• Switch roles.

Everything that happens is a part of the whole configuration of signs. The physical, vocal, and verbal actions interact as they interpenetrate. This weaving depends on a particular clarity. There must be no rough edges to the sounds, movements or words. The timing of each expression must be crisply what it is. Only then can the performers sense one another.

Awareness/Emotion

By far the biggest hurdle in all of this is to maintain body awareness while involved with language or emotion. Emotion may surface due to a sensation or a thought. A movement, posture, idea or memory may trigger emotion. We hook into emotion ferociously, and blind ourselves to the moment-to-moment sensations of the body. Since we identify with, and believe we *are* the emotion, we feel the need to either relate to the emotion all-out or repress it. We rant, rave, moan, groan, laugh, cry, tremble, scream, tense up. If we savor the ongoing moments of these actions, moment to moment, notice them in detail, then we can stay both in our body and open for change. If we get seduced by emotion only, then noticing stops. Change stops. We get stuck.

"But emotion is in the body," we might say, "How can I leave my body when I'm in emotion?" We don't actually leave our body (that's impossible), but we do stop paying attention to it. So in this exercise, we pay attention to the body by not moving it at all as we sound or talk. And for our purposes, it must not move *at all*. We're strict about that. Intended stillness demands attention and that's how we stay in the body. Seems funny doesn't it?

Our body doesn't want to be still. It fidgets. Everybody has his or her own peculiar choreography, especially when experiencing arousal. Some of us talk with our hands waving around like flags, or poke them into space like pop-up books. Some of us rock back and forth on our feet, change our stance, move from place to place, look around, or realign our neck in relation to our shoulders. This list can go on and on.

In order to keep the body still, we must pay attention to it. We must be *in* it. Completely. As soon as our attention sways, even for a second, fidgeting will resume. Of course, there's nothing wrong with fidgets in themselves. Noticed fidgets offer an abundance of information and style. But unintentional fidgets result in a limited palette of both experience and expression.

Speech is action and movement.

Say "Wait." Feel it. Notice the lips puckering to form the "w" sound. The air blowing out between the lips. The lips pulling back and the sides of the tongue on the "ai." The tip of the tongue on the "t." What else do you notice when you say, "Wait."?

The Sounder, Speaker and Mover are in a musical relationship. They're noticing the rhythms, pulses, retards, punctuations. They're composing, as any musicians would. Time is in their bodies. They're listening to one another through their senses; watching their collective time, space and shape patterns. They sense how every moment of their action hits up against, passes through, circles around, coincides with, and slips in between their partner's moments of action. All three hear the patterns of sound and see the patterns of image. They shape the improvisation together. They serve the music. They hold their own impulses with a loose hand. Direct responses unfold. The material they notice, hear, see, and feel determines what they do next.

Each movement of the Mover, sound of the Sounder, word and word parts of the Speaker weaves into the tapestry just as a weaver knows how the color, size and texture of the current stitch relates to the whole pattern. The performers begin to develop this mutual weave which precludes the possibility of anyone spinning off into their own world unaware of their partners.

In order for this type of noticing to happen, each member of the group must do more than simply observe each other's action. They must feel it internally, sense it: notice and "get it" simultaneously. Immediately. They "get it" through their bodies, not from time-consuming interpretation or evaluation.

A musical relationship allows performers a more spacious relationship. They hear each other in time. They don't have to pounce on each other's content right away. They begin to see how images, feelings, stories may contrast, stretch, and poke out from their dreamlike, surreal, super-real imagination.

13D. Solo:
Separate Sound, Movement and Language

• Now, let's work with this in solo. Everyone, find a place for yourself on the floor (it may be where you already are). You're not confined to that place. It's a place for you to begin from consciously. You are, of course, free to move throughout the room.

• You may either move, sound, or speak. In keeping with the day, you may only do one mode of expression at a time.

• Play with time and order, particularly. For example, you might shift rapidly from one mode to another. A sound could lead to language, then back into sound which, then, suggests to you a movement, which calls for another bit of language. Let movement, speech, and sound interact. One will lead to another, but they all work separately.

At first, this may seem like an extraordinarily awkward situation: dividing up expression into discreet parts and still trying to get a flow out of it. It feels self-contradicting. But with practice, it works. Just as moving water in a stream bounces off a rock to cascade down to a still pond to get mixed up in an eddy to whip out over a falls to tumble over some river pebbles to make a break for it through a narrow channel, even this peculiar behavior we are doing has an ongoing flow. Experience is going on and on, sometimes expressing through movement, sometimes sound, sometimes language. It's always moving water. It's always self-expressing.

Content is going on and on, too. Sometimes expressed with gesture, sometimes sound, sometimes speech. The content doesn't begin anew each time the mode of expression changes. Rather, the modes of expression, each in turn, take the content one notch further. One mode calls the next, calling, wanting, asking for it.

Adherence to this strict separation of expressive modes forces the students to work differently. They are propelled into expanded awareness. Surprises happen. A small idea, image or story, may lift to become a multi-dimensional, multi-faceted narrative.

Switching modes while continuing the content flow changes the preconceived relationship between movement, sounds and words. Each element can depict an image differently. Each draws from different aspects of mind.

Continue practicing until you can smooth this out and it makes bodily sense to you. Then, we'll bring this technique back into relationship.

13E. Trios:
Separate Sound, Movement and Language

• Everyone, find the partners that you worked with before, or just get into trios.

• Following our progression today, each of you may either move, sound or speak. Just as before, you may only do one at a time. Within these restraints, you collaborate to build a scene.

• At any time, you may be in the same mode or different modes. You may pause, be still and silent, whenever appropriate.

• Sometimes do what one, or both, of your partners is doing. Join them. Add bulk to the image. If a strong situation occurs, stay with it. Stay involved.

• Remember, you must be completely still when you are speaking or sounding.

Now, that's a lot to keep track of. Not only do you have to be a fluent sounder, mover and speaker, you have to keep the modes discreetly separate while, at the same time, building a scene with your partners.

You have to pay attention to everything they're doing while you're paying attention to everything you're doing.

Every action, no matter who makes it, enters and leaves the flow of others action and is an ordering of energy. If you don't get involved in ownership issues ("This is my action and that is yours"), but accept every contribution into the improvisation as "what is," then there's really very little difference between partnering and solo work. Either solo or with partner(s), you're part of the river participating in its flow.

Every time a student adds action into the scene, whether it be movement, sound or speech, they, of course, want the action to be noticed by their partners. So, their action must be noticeable. Their intention must interact with their awareness of what others are doing. They must gauge the scene and then make adjustments to make sure their input is receivable and received. Contrast helps. Their action, even if it's a logical step in the progression of events, may have to be different from what's going on in rhythm, shape, space, or dynamic. Through contrast, they feel themselves in relation to the others. And the audience receives clear, sharp images. They also have to be able to tolerate the scrutiny and attention which will be the result of entering/interrupting others' work. The more they think of themselves as "an element" rather than "me, trying to get attention" the more they'll be able to enter smoothly.

Within the flow of an improvisation, situations and patterns always arise. Suppose a trio finds themselves in a two-and-one situation, or, suppose they're all doing the same thing, moving in the same way, or sounding the same motif, or developing a monologue collaboratively. As in previous exercises, they're encouraged to stay with situations, not as shallow experiences, but with full commitment, full belief. This commitment, this staying, will give the scene depth and take it beyond normalcy, beyond safety into impact. It will push everybody, the performers and the audience, into an altered reality.

13F. Performance Score: Separate Sound, Movement and Language

• Everyone off the floor except one trio. Now, we'll watch each trio that has been practicing together. Start fresh. Don't try to use any material from your previous improvisations.

The book of signs opens. The content and the form are intentionally exposed. Students not only intend to communicate with each other, they intend to communicate with the audience. This resolve affects the improvisation; the volume and quality of the voices sharpen, shaping and spacing all change. The content lifts, too.

Beyond Self/Big Awareness

14A. Sensation to Action
14B. Circle Transformation
14C. Transformation, Two Lines
14D. Directed Shift/Transform/Develop
14E. Witnessed Shift/Transform/Develop
14F. Performance Score: One Minute of All Possible Sounds

We watch, don't we? Each other, trees, birds and wars. We watch ourselves going through the gestures of living, making the appropriate or inappropriate grunts, groans, grasps and growls. Even when we're unaware of watching, we watch. We wake in the morning and we know how our night was. "Slept like a log." Who did? The watcher? Or we could say the watching? Watching watched me sleep.

W hat is probably the most basic exercise in this whole training comes up today. Why on the fourteenth day and not the first? We've been laying groundwork, stilling minds, coming to inhabit our bodies, prodding memories, igniting imaginations and resurrecting feelings. Yes, even watching ourselves watching ourselves.

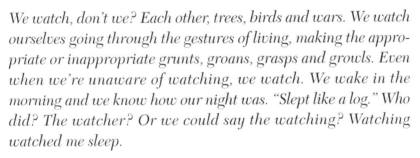

14A. Sensation to Action

• Everyone, lie down. Relax. With each breath, relax even more into the floor. Place as much space as possible between all of your bones. Beginning at your feet and slowly moving upward, scan your body. If you notice any tension, let it go. With each exhalation, relax your mind as well. Relax any tension present in the form of thought. Quiet yourself. Quiet your brain. Melt it. Mush it. Relax it. Lie there. No noise . . .

• Notice the sensation of your breath. Don't change it or do anything to it. Just notice it. Notice the details of the experience. As your attention moves over your limbs and trunk, notice the separate sensation in your body. Anything. Maybe a tight spot, or itch, or heaviness or lightness, of some body part. Or a hollowness. I'm using words now to talk to you but notice sensation without talking to yourself, without language. Just feel it.

• Notice another sensation, whatever comes into your attention. Again don't do anything about it. Just watch it. Do the same with another . . . and another . . .

• Again, notice a sensation. Allow that sensation to inspire feeling, affect your state of mind. Don't worry where the feeling comes from. It's either your imagination, or memory, or a combination of both. Do this again. And again . . .

• Notice another sensation, whatever comes into your attention. And accompanying feeling. This time I would like you to move into that feeling/sensation. Explore whatever kind of movement that feeling/sensation calls up. Play with the movement. No reservations. Let it take you for a ride. Sensation, feeling, action. Sensation, feeling, action.

• Stop. Return to lying down in neutral.

• Again notice a sensation and allow that sensation to affect your state of mind and guide you into movement. Follow the feeling/action. Stop. Return to neutral.

• Notice a sensation again, and again, allow the sensation to lead you to feeling/action. Now, stay with feeling/action. As you play with the movement, continue to notice new sensations as they arise. Let these new sensations lead you into new movement.

• Now, bring someone who is near you into your awareness. Don't relate to them, just become aware of their existence nearby. Continue following your sensation/feeling/action loop . . .

Notice more detail of the behavior of your partner. Allow what you notice— the specifics of their actions, as well as, their inner condition—to affect what you do. Don't get pulled away from your inner awareness. Follow your own experience.

We begin with the intention of noticing sensations in the body and not acting on them. We just watch them: we practice control. Not scratching the itch. Not stretching the cramp. Not filling the hollowness. We allow what is, to be what is, without wanting or needing change. This ability is fundamental to our training. Everything else builds on top of it in layers.

We're not interpreting these sensory experiences. We're not creating images or story. We're not talking to ourselves at all. Our language mind remains quiet.

Language tends to take us away from moment-to-moment body experience. It doesn't have to. With practice, a student can be in the moment-to-moment body experience of languaging. For now, we practice the direct, unmediated, experiencing of the body.

Impulsive reactions cloud awareness. Don't react, remain aware continually, without interruption. By not reacting, by just noticing, we come to know the "noticer" as separate from the experience being noticed. This builds internal muscle. We're not whipped around in the wind anymore; the phenomenological world becomes something to watch. From calm strength, we're able to choose responses.

Towards the end of this exercise, our intention changes: we respond to the sensations we notice; we move into, with, from, or around them. Our actions are conscious, chosen. We can, just as well, choose not to.

Picture this scenario. Laura sits in a very small room. The room has two doors. The two doors face each other. Laura is sitting silently with her friend Emily. Emily gets up and leaves through one of the doors. Laura sees Emily leave (sensation). She interprets Emily's action as rejection and immediately feels abandoned (feeling). She reflexively acts on the feeling. Laura runs to the door, but it's locked. She bangs and bangs on the door. She screams, kicks and yells (action). Laura doesn't notice that Emily has returned through the other door.

How would you direct this scene? What other choices does Laura have?

Braiding

When you make a braid you take three, or more, clumps of hair and intertwine them until they become interconnected and inseparable. They loose their individual identity and become one braid. Similarly, we separate objects of awareness and explore them with immaculate attention. Later, these objects of awareness, sensation, feeling, intention and action (whether movement, vocalization or speech) integrate and become one thing—one unified action, full of sensation and feeling, motivated by intention.

If the performer's attention is on her experience, if her mind and body are in the same place, her inner and outer experience will match, and she will enter the field of universal expression. She will be relating, to *the* experience, not *her* experience.

Within universal expression, we hold conscious action lightly and fiercely at the same time. Lightly enough, so we can continually notice the details of form, shape, quality of feeling and meaning. Fiercely enough, so we are 100% committed to each moment of action.

What's the difference between "self-indulgent" expression (action that is too personal) and universal expression? Intention? Not necessarily. Awareness? Yes, absolutely.

S hift, transform and develop.

These are the three ways we proceed through improvisational experience. In Day Eight, we began to investigate the transformation process. We transformed the content of an action while keeping the form consistent. Now, we're going to transform both the content and the form of an action. This transformation process requires an encompassing awareness. There's a lot to notice. Sensation, feeling, and action integrate, simultaneously and with exquisite detail.

14B. Circle Transformation

FIRST FORM:

• Let's get into a large circle. We're going to work with sound and movement. One of you, A, begins by standing in front of another, B, and repeating a sound and movement gesture with a clear beginning and end. At the end of the gesture, before you start it again, there's a slight pause. You almost return to neutral but not entirely. You hold a bit of the feeling, then repeat the gesture. After a few cycles, you'll set up a pulsing rhythm. We'll maintain this pulsing rhythm throughout this exercise.

• A continues to repeat the sound and movement phrase until B picks it up, mirrors it. Then B, while rhythmically repeating the gesture, travels into the center of the circle. As B travels, s/he, step by step, increment by increment, transforms the sound and movement simultaneously until both the form and content are different than what s/he began with. Then, B travels over to another person standing in the circle, C, and stands in front of C, repeating the newly transformed gesture until C picks it up and begins to travel into the circle transforming it. (B takes C's place in the circle.) The process continues until everyone has had several turns.

SECOND FORM:

• Let's break up into small circles, four or five people in each one. Continue this process. If any of you sees one of your partners slipping out of the transformation flow—either by adding something to the action that was not inherent in the previous one or repeating the action rather than changing it incrementally—stop him and let him begin again.

THIRD FORM:

Break into twos. Stand about five feet apart. A gives a sound and movement to B. B transforms it and gives the new action to A. A transforms that and gives his or her new action to B. They continue transforming, giving each other actions back and forth.

Remember those little flip books. You'd quickly flick through the pages and the cartoon man inside would step by step, increment by increment, perform some kind of act. There would usually be a surprise at the end. If we settled on a page, any page, and just looked at it, it would be a unique drawing, only ever so slightly different from the one before it and the one after it. The shape of the man's body would be a little different and so would his state of mind. Page by page. If we looked at the first page and then flipped right to the last, we'd probably see a "shift," two unrelated actions, each having different form and content. All of the inside pages show us how the little man got from the first page to the last. Step by step.

Transformation works very much like a flip book. Each individual pulse of sound and movement corresponds to a page, the shape and quality of the action slightly changes, as does the shape and quality of the sound. The inner condition, state of mind, or feeling shifts slightly from pulse to pulse, too. The expression on the face, indicating the state of mind, changes incrementally move by move, page by page. Each action is the child of the action before it and the parent of the one following. Everything in the present action is inherent or suggested in the preceding action.

Transformation differs from a flip book because the images in the

Transformation

flip book are static poses. Once we begin a transformation, we never stop. Our actions of transformation move rhythmically, pulsing, always almost returning to neutral, but not quite.

This technique may be the most challenging in the training. It insists that the thinking mind be quiet, that sensation, feeling, and action integrate into a loop of experience. A three-headed horse bolting into one new reality after another. The mind must pay attention to all the details involved. What's going on in one action cues the next action. The performer should not be hatching ideas, thinking, planning, or identifying.

When a student pulses through sound and movement actions, the jump out of the incremental flow is a jolt. Everyone watching feels the shock in their own bodies. It's as if a page were torn out of the flip book. All of a sudden, with no warning.

An action or sound appears from out of nowhere, unconnected to the one before.

The performer sinks into a repetition, the same action over and over again.

The performer speeds up or slows down, but the skeletal form doesn't change.

The performer enlarges or shrinks the action, but content doesn't change.

Or just the sound transforms.

Or just the movement.

Or just the feeling.

When any of the above happens, the student should back up a move, or two, and go at it again. A moment of thought interfered with the student's attention to internal experience.

Transformation leads to wildness. Given the wheel, the body (sensation-feeling-action) will drive itself off the normal road, down embankments into raging, or sublime feeling, through dark tunnels of demons and resurrections, and end up on top of ecstatic mountains peaks. Only hesitation, doubt, or a lack of willingness puts on the brakes.

We're continuing with transformation. However, now we go faster.

14C. Transformation, Two Lines

• Form two lines, about eight feet apart and facing each other.

• The first person in one line approaches the first person in the other line by incrementally transforming a sound and movement action with each step. That person quickly mirrors the action (the first person who walked over takes his place in line) and proceeds toward the second person in the opposite line transforming the action as she goes. That person mirrors the action and transforms it as she travels toward the second person in the other line. We'll go up and down the lines this way until the transformations are clear and smooth. We'll work up and down the lines very quickly. Remember, both the form and the content change incrementally . . .

• Take a step or two towards each other. We'll cut the space down so the transformations must happen more quickly.

• After this round, we'll continue to pull the lines closer until the transformations happen in only three or four clean moves.

Transformations may be intimidating. Students are so afraid of doing it wrong, either skipping, missing or imposing, that they end up spinning their wheels. Once they "get it" the process skips along.

Now, students are ready to greet it all head on: **Shift, Transform, Develop.**

14D. Directed Shift/Transform/Develop

• Everyone, in pairs. One of you will be the Director, and the other will be the Actor. The Director can say three words, Shift, Transform, or Develop. When the Actor hears one of these directions, he responds accordingly.

• Directors, please limit your direction to only those three words, although you can say them in any order. But, you can only say, "Develop," when your actor is transforming. (They automatically develop after every shift.)

• The actors can work with any combination of movement, sound, and language: movement only, sound and movement, sound only, and language with or without movement. Even combining language and sound is possible.

• If the actor hears the word, "Shift," she abruptly stops the action and does something else. She changes her mind and approaches an action which is very different from all the shifts preceding it.

• Actor, if you hear the word, "Develop," while you're transforming, take some care to frame that moment. Notice its physical composition (the action and sensations of the body) and the exact quality of the mind (intention within the action). Then, explore the condition and situation (if any) within that frame. Don't add to it, or subtract. Your timing may have been regular while transforming, but when you're developing, your timing becomes whatever is relevant.

• If the director says, "Transform," then similarly, the actor should frame that moment, set the action with a specific beginning and end, and begins to alter it. With a pulsing rhythm, s/he incrementally changes the sound and movement of the action. If you were speaking when the director said, "Transform," then begin to deconstruct the language into sound, with whatever bit of gesture you were engaged in. If you were moving, then add sound to the movement and transform the two simultaneously.

• Continue until I say, "Stop." Then, Director tell the Actor your experience of their physical and psychological range; whether their shifts, transformations and developments were clear. Share notes. See if you travelled the same road.

• Reverse roles.

Jess stands in neutral. Kevin says, "Shift." Jess makes shapes in space with his finger while humming a lullaby-like melody. Jess explores this for a while, melting into the soothing quality of his actions. Kevin says, "Transform." Jess's arm had just arched over his head and his vocal sound at that moment was an upturned "uhm." Jess turns his attention to the inside of that moment (framing it) and beginning with the arm arch and the upturning "uhm," he pulses the movement and sound transformation. After a few moments, Kevin says, "Shift." Jess stops the transforming process and shifts his mind to a different condition and situation: he talks about sunsets in Utah with a squeaky voice, as if he's in pain, slowly pacing back and forth. Kevin doesn't say anything for a long time. Jess stays within the form. He doesn't change it. He develops it. Not bigger. Not squeakier. His pacing remains slow.

Because Kevin doesn't make him shift, Jess has time to give over to his condition more and more. He becomes what he's doing. Totally. 100%. Kevin says, "Transform." Jess had just said, "Frontier," and his right knee was up high in the air. Jess frames this moment of action, deconstructs the word "frontier," ("frontier . . . frotee . . . roti . . . ") while picking up one knee after another, higher and higher. His mood has changed. He's something like a cheerleader, and on the next move he's something like an animal, and on the next move he's some kind of demon. And he goes on and on allowing his psyche (memory, imagination, feeling) to interact with his body (sensation) and propel him into ever-changing realms of consciousness. During one of the transformation steps, Jess swings his arms to the right. He's very tense. His fingers dart into space. His face bursts open. His weight is on his right foot, and he's saying, "Shum." Kevin says, "Develop." Jess focuses on that moment and explores it. His hands dart here and there around him. He's tense. Weight alternates from foot to foot, moving around the room. He repeats the sound, "Shum." He appears frantic, caught in some kind of turmoil. Rodent-like. Again, Kevin lets Jess stay there a long time before he moves him along.

Lifting the Burden

Being directed may liberate many students. They can freely engage with their experience, knowing the burden of engineering material is carried by the director.

The director protects the actor from the tyranny of his own judgments. When the actor is called upon to change, he's reflecting what the director likes, found interesting or absorbing, or doesn't.

Suppose, we normally would fail to notice the way the fingers spread when we grab for something. Our director might say, "Develop," just as the fingers were spreading. We would then have to notice what our action was at that very moment. If we're limited to the exploration of the spreading of fingers, then that action, which under normal conditions, might slip by unnoticed, becomes a conduit for curiosity.

Practicing "Shift, Transform and Develop" accustoms students to noticing moments of experience. Being directed gives them the experience of someone else's insight and opinions on the work.

Next, the student will self-direct. Not by saying "Shift," "Transform," or "Develop," to themselves, but by following their own rhythms, impulses, and attractions.

14E. Witnessed Shift/Transform/Develop

• Let's change partners to get a different perspective on things.

• One of you will improvise within the process of shift, transform or develop, and the other will watch. If, at any time, the watcher is unclear as to what the actor is doing—shifting, transforming or developing—the watcher may stop the actor and ask. The actor clarifies, not by talking about it, but by adjusting her actions, and then continues on . . .

• Switch roles.

Imagine a percussionist sitting among an assortment of drums, cymbals, clackers, shakers, bells, whistles, triangles, and rain makers. She begins to improvise, gently rubbing her hands together. Suddenly, she slaps one of the drums, over and over, and on and on, and on and on. Abruptly, she stops. There's a pause. A silence. She reaches for one of the small bells and begins a rhythm with her left hand. After a few moments, she adds a melodious beat on one of the drums. Both voices, the bell and the drum talk to each other first small, gently. Gradually, the sound builds and new patterns are introduced to the rhythm. She continues the motif and moves both hands to a conga drum. The pattern is very complex.

Knowing When

How does the percussionist know when to stop hitting the drum? How does she know to pause, to be silent? How does she know to pick-up again with a bell?

How does the improvisor know when to shift, transform or develop?

She doesn't, in a thinking sense. She doesn't evaluate, speculate, desire or fear.

The percussionist and the improvisor pay attention. They listen, or stand by. They watch the event from the inside. They follow their actions: they allow the sounds to come to their consciousness, sensations to be noticed, feelings to manifest, images to occur, the memories to become realized, and thoughts to erupt. Of course, the freer the percussionist and the improviser are, the more able they are to stand by without interference. The more skilled they are, the more they can live through their instrument, whether it's the drums and clackers or the body itself. Freedom doesn't often show itself on the fourteenth day of the training. Students may have to say to themselves, "Shift," "Transform," or "Develop." They may have to fight their self-consciousness into this process. They may not quite trust their impulses, trust that they, in fact, do know what to do next.

Each student has to come to terms with each condition on some level, before he can shift out of it. A student must have experienced the condition before they can free themselves from it. Each condition has to be lived; it becomes something else and, then, something else again through the process.

Inside of self-consciousness, students can notice the next step. Rather than fight against struggle, they may stay with struggle and develop it. Or, they may transform the condition's experience, and work through the inside of it. Or they may shift out of it.

If the student really shifts, transforms, or develops, with no holding back, she will be liberated from what held her back.

It's been a hard day's work. Every one of today's exercises challenged the students. Each demanded absolute focus. Each was a baby step pointing toward vast terrains of awareness. It's time to release the tension.

14F. Performance Score:
One Minute of All Possible Sounds

• Let's sit in a circle. One by one, we'll each take a turn and sound as many different qualities of sound possible in a minute of time. I've got a stopwatch here. I'll start you and stop you. Remember sounds carry feeling. Open your mouth. Step aside and let your body voice itself.

Shift, transform or develop. Three choices. Simple. Continue doing what you're doing. Stop what you're doing and do something else. Or, change what you're doing until it becomes something else. What appears so simple, in fact, demands a miracle: a quiet mind, an expanded awareness, a willingness to leap into the unknown, and an integrated body and mind. A most possible miracle.

Freedom

15A. Episodes
15B. Face the Music
15C. Shift with Initiator
15D. Solo Shift
15E. Performance Score: Solo Shift

A raggedy man totters in the subway door, half in and half out. Enraged, he shouts and screams unintelligible words at the passengers. He's wild.

The little girl squeals, laughs and screams, at an exploding pitch. She kicks her small feet in the water and gasps as the water sprays her in the face. She's wild.

The lovers claw at each other, rip off clothes, pull, squeeze and jerk at each other's limbs and torsos. One mouth is in the other's. They're wild.

We could say that these people have lost their minds. Whether the content of their actions is playful, ecstatic or hostile, their experience draws from energy broken free from thought.

The man in the subway is untethered. He has no tie to safety. He's lost his awareness and his condition is dangerous.

The little girl is untethered, too. Let's assume there's a adult with her to keep her out of danger.

The lovers are tethered. Their safety is tied to the conventions of lovemaking. Of course, if one of them deviates from the conventions, they negotiate. If negotiations fail and disparity persists, there's danger.

In **Episodes,** students approach wildness. The constraints of the form keep them out of danger, safe.

15A. Episodes

• Everyone walk. Find a common pace.

• In a few moments, one of you will stop walking and throw a fit, have a tantrum, an outburst. The fit must be expressed as a travelling *sound and movement* form. As soon as a fit begins, everyone else stops walking and watches.

• "Mad person," let loose. Keep the sound and movement linked and travel with it, cover space. Remember every movement is sounded and every

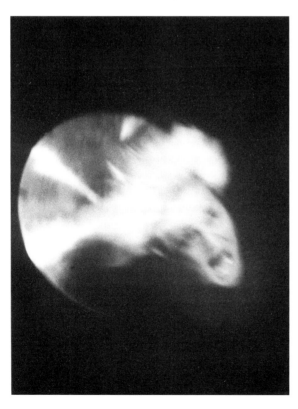

sound is moved. You may pause in stillness and silence, but let yourself go where you have never been before. You can't plan it. Don't even try. When you've completed your outburst, pause for a moment, let the experience resonate, then resume your walk.

• Watchers, notice the details of the fit. See how it moves, listen to how it sounds, feel how it feels. Remain still until the "fitter" finishes, then begin to walk when she does.

• After everybody has had a turn or two at this you can join the person who is doing the fit. Do what they're doing just as they do it. No tempering. Join fits that are unfamiliar to you . . .

• Eliminate the walking. The fits come

one right after another. You're either still and silent, or you're doing what someone else is doing, or you're initiating a new fit. If you're still and silent, pause in the final shape of your last expression. Don't go to neutral. Expand your awareness to include the entire ensemble in your frame of perception. Look and listen. Relate to space, shape, and time. Only one fit can happen at a time. If a new fit is introduced, everyone pauses; only if someone joins you, may you continue. Let the fits be responses to the ones that came before.

The surest way a child can throw an adult into mental chaos is to throw a tantrum. Parents, siblings, teachers, doctors, therapists, experts in child development, all rack their brains figuring out the best approach. Should they ignore the child or should they put the child in a room and lock the door? Should they go away? Should they buckle under and give the child what he wants? Should they show affection? Show anger? Calm the child down? Mirror the wild behavior? Whatever the tactic, their aim is to turn the tantrum off and restore "peace."

Why? In the wild tantrum state, awareness is lost. The released energy floods a large part, if not all, of sensory perception. Somebody may get hurt. In **Episodes**, students are asked to specifically combine sound and movement while travelling through the room. That means they must pay attention to what they're doing, how they structure their expression and they must remain aware of the others in the room, too. Their wildness is contained. To that degree they're aware. Awareness dams the flood, contains it. There's no overflow into danger.

Every exercise in this training expands awareness. Awareness is see-ing. We use the term "blind rage" meaning sightless, out-of- control rage. As soon as rage becomes insightful rage, it boils within an awareness con-text. The one who rages knows what's going on. She is safe to rage. No one will get hurt. The more awareness is expanded, the more capacity i.e., control, the student has to unleash, uncork, and liberate wildness.

Wildness has nothing to do with content, but is defined by freedom. Feeling free, we feel unencumbered. We're not advocating a "wildness" theater or even tantrums. But, until a student can uninhibitedly express her every feeling, she can't really know if her constraints are from aesthetic or practical choice, or from fear of reprisal.

> *John releases his line. The fish pulls away and for a few moments swims wildly toward freedom. Then, John starts winding the reel, tightening the line, wrestling the fish into shore. Then, he lets it out again, and again the fish takes off, and again John reels it in. Back and forth, release and tighten, release and tighten. They fight with one another. All the time the fish is coming closer in to shore, until finally John lifts it from the water, frees it from the hook and sends it back to the sea.*

John alternates between control and letting go. We do the same thing. From the release of **Episodes**, we'll reel our attention to the rigors of listening.

15B. Face the Music

• Find a partner. One of you, A, begins by tapping a rhythmic pattern on the floor with your feet. The other, B, repeats the pattern. If B has difficulty repeating the pattern, A repeats it until B gets it. Don't discuss it. Talk to each other through your feet. Now, B taps a pattern on the floor and A repeats it. Switch roles back and forth, each time developing more complex patterns. Do this without looking at your, or your partner's, feet.

• The next step: Instead of tapping your feet, move different body parts—arms, little finger or knee—and do a rhythmic pattern that your partner then repeats. Again, alternate back and forth while increasing complexity.

• Step three: Change the expression of your face rhythmically. Have these facial expressions express changing inner states. Alternate turns and, again, go for increasingly complicated patterns.

• Make it hard for each other.

In many cases, music is simply sequential rhythmic patterns and silence. Musical relationships exist whether we notice them or not. Time patterns are always going on whether we notice them or not. One action follows another whether we notice that or not.

Face the Music is a "practice your scales" and focus exercise. The sensory receptors' ability to distinguish more and more complicated information increases with practice. So does the ability to translate that information into action. Students experience that action embedded in a moment-to-moment chain of change. Any distractions from the task at hand result in missed beats, lost information.

We control, mask, immobilize and don't feel the face more than any other part of their body. In Step Three of this exercise, the expressions of the face reflect inner condition. To change these expressions in a rhythmical pattern while truly being "in" them, requires the student to, in a sense, step back from his face and feel it as separate from him. It is an object with bones, muscles and flesh. It moves. He can dance with his face.

Both **Episodes** and **Face the Music** work at the underpinnings of improvisation. The first invites freedom, the second, control.

15C. Shift with Initiator

• Find a partner. You're going to do a "shift" exercise together. You're both in the same world, or scene, and you're shifting your actions more or less simultaneously. However, one of you will always shift first, as the primary shifter, and the other will always shift slightly afterwards as the secondary shifter. Your shifts are always a response.

• Keep this perspective. You're making scenes together. The primary shifter provides half of the scene. The secondary shifter completes the other half.

• Even though you're in the same scene and responding to each other, your forms of expression must differ. If the primary shifter is only moving, the secondary shifter must either speak or sound. If the primary shifter is using sound and movement, the secondary shifter has the options of sounding from a still body, or moving without sound or speech.

- Here are the options:
  Movement only
  Sound only
  Speech only
  Sound and movement
  Movement and speech
  Speech and sound
  Movement, sound and speech

- You'll do this for ten minutes, discuss it and then switch primary and secondary roles.

You're walking down the street. A car screeches. You respond.
The stew boils over. You respond.
There's a knock on the door. You respond.
The phone rings. You respond.
A stranger says, "How are you?" You respond.

These are ordinary circumstances. But how about these?

A child flies by your front door.
Someone is laughing uncontrollably an inch from your face.
A door, hanging in space, is opening and closing over and over
*   again.*
Someone spins in circles next to you, making wordless
*   stuttering sounds.*
Someone kneels at your feet, holding his breath, smiling.

Responses to less ordinary happenings need not take any more time than responses to ordinary ones. Quickness requires only innocence, which we had when we were young; life could contain just about anything. Anything was believable.

What makes any primary or secondary actions "real?" When a child flies by your door, what makes that real? Belief. If the student believes that the child is flying by their door, then the child is flying by their door. Really. Response erupts from belief. Not as an interesting idea, but as truth at that moment.

In Day Eleven, the **It Responds** exercise prepared the student for this type of sophisticated structure. In **Shift with Initiator** both the primary and the secondary shifters are responding to each other. The scenario flows, one scene leading to the next. Students have to focus on content and building "scenes." They hold the content lightly so that the moments of action don't have to connect literally, but can stretch beyond the borders of normal.

Content varies from student to student. Some students thrive in fantasy, surreal, and non-sequitur realms. Others are more political, or psychological. Some draw from natural history, science, or myth. Some are funny, some serious. Some are more kinetic, some, more vocal. Some have a way with language. The entire universe is in the studio, embodied as students.

On occasion, a student wants to be normal. They want to respond in a "normal" way. Once one's awareness expands, "normal" becomes nuances, detail, and awesome peculiarities. Everything is normal, and everything isn't. Normal isn't normal anymore and every perspective is heightened.

Reframe

Reframing is another inroad into the imagination. Through her action, the secondary shifter may *re-frame*, or change the meaning, of the primary shifter's actions. She can paint another picture around the action to change its context and meaning.

For example:

*A is rapidly and desperately blowing on her hands to cool them
   off as if they are too hot.*
B reframes by selling her as a new kind of air-conditioner.
*A is moving slow-motion, obviously euphoric, describing his
   gravity-less atmosphere.*
B reframes by aggressively playing him as a pin ball machine.

As in **It Responds**, the secondary shifts, here, are required to be
expressively different. In addition to the options listed above in the exercise, they must differ formally in time, space, shape and tension. As experience accumulates, this just happens. B wants to "sense" their action,
clearly defined, in relation to A's. Students are drawn to the strength of
counterpoint and difference.
   Remember:

Everything your partner does is perfect.
Your partner is perfectly being himself, always.
Make whatever your partner does work.
*Your partner's action is only action. It's not totally his, and is
   certainly not yours. Action is just action.*

Also, remember:

Everything you do is perfect.
You are perfectly being yourself, always.
What you do works.
Your action is only action. Action is not a person's being.

On the one hand, we talk about "no separation" and on the other
"clear boundaries." These are different ways of saying "separation." These
are contradictory if we confuse action with identity. Neither we, nor our
partners, are what we do. We're awareness. In awareness there's no "I,"
no separation of I, me, mine, you, yours. At the "We" or the "I" level,
separation enters and boundaries between who I am and who you are
become important. In this theater, we play freely with both constructs:
"We," "You," and "I" as fiction, and the self we normally experience. We

aren't rigidly bound into one conception of self.

A student can judge, criticize, be confused about, or question her partner's action. Or she can accept her partner's action as perfect, perfectly what it is. How can it be anything else, really? As identification slips away from action, the student perceives all action, hers and her partner's, as impersonal and unowned. With ownership comes judgment, evaluation, comparison. Without ownership, each action stands perfectly.

15D. Solo Shifts

• Separate from your partner and practice shifts on your own. You have no director. The timing of your shifts is up to you. Don't say "shift" to yourself. Just shift whenever the impulse strikes. Remember, the shifts must be very different in form from each other.

• Now, work with this perspective. Begin with a primary shift. At some point respond with a secondary shift. As that becomes primary to the next response, make the next shift. Remember the boundless frame.

Partners with Me

We're always in partnership with ourselves. It's evident when we see people on the street talking to themselves. We consider that aberrant behavior. But we talk to ourselves too, don't we? If we have any sense, we just don't do it noticeably. So who's talking and to whom? Isn't the talker talking to the listener? Then the listener responds as talker, talking to the listener, who before was the talker. So the talker and the listener are one and two at the same time. Primary, secondary, primary, secondary . . .

In all improvisations, every moment responds to the one before, whether they're micro-moments inside a developing shift, or the shifts, themselves. One moment talks to the next.

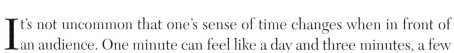

15E. Performance Score: Solo Shifts

• Everyone please leave the floor and sit in a line as audience. You'll each do a performance of shifts, one, two or three minutes, your choice. We'll begin at one end of the line and continue in order.

• We'll pass a watch. You'll each time the person who proceeds you. When you get up for your turn, tell your timer how many minutes you want. Timer, call out, "Stop," loud and clear when the minute, or minutes, run out.

It's not uncommon that one's sense of time changes when in front of an audience. One minute can feel like a day and three minutes, a few blinks. It depends on the accompanying qualities of pain or pleasure. And that depends on whether the student is directly experiencing or not. In direct experience, pain and pleasure, like freedom and control, normal and abnormal, become irrelevant.

A student's choice of one, two, or three minutes generally reflects her *anticipated* pain or pleasure. It's not always that logical. These time choices in themselves are subject to exploration. Some go for three minutes just so they can then have the opportunity to explore that experience of uncomfortableness. Others may go for one minute because they don't want to have too much pleasure.

Examples of feedback on solos:

Instead of reporting on what you're doing, be what you're
*   doing.*
You shift prematurely. Don't rush. Immerse yourself.
Have your shifts come from your body energy, not your head.
You're thinking up your next shift while you're still doing your
*   last. Relax and let the shifts take care of themselves.*
If it's fear you're feeling, deal with it. Investigate it. Move into
*   it. The sensations. Build a story around it.*
You're complicating things. Let each shift stay where it began.
*   Don't add to it by making it more of anything. Accept it.*
'Fess up. If some feeling is blocking your energy and fun, use it
*   as material for shifts.*
I see your outside, what you're doing. I want to see your inside,
*   what you're being.*
Relax, relax, relax.

We're exploding the boundaries between infancy and adulthood,
lucidity and lunacy, humanity and bestiality, banal and sacred states. The
experience of entering and surviving these states grants permission to
explore even further, continually expanding the limits of the conceivable
and the expressible. Our frame
expands to include all universal experience as equal and the
same, within awareness.

Relationship

16A. Space Between
16B. Chords
16C. Ensemble: Walk/Run/"Ah"
16D. Shift By Interruption
16E. 1/3–1/3–1/3
16F. Angels
16G. Performance Score: Disparate Dialogue

We shape our experience?
Isn't that how we see the world?
As shapes of things?
We fill in space,
with shape.
We see space within shape.
We name shape
as tree, cookie, smile,
sadness, house or mathematics.

Often we don't name, we just sense. We sense the space/shape of our body, through motion, kinetically. We sense the space/shape outside of our body, through sight and hearing. We may sense the space/shape inside and outside our body as inseparable. One isn't without the other, since the shape of the body affects the space around it, and vice-versa.

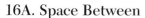

16A. Space Between

• Everyone, spread out in the room and find a place to stand.

• Your feet are shoulder width apart, arms relaxed by your sides. Take the next few breaths to quiet yourself, rid the tension from your body. Stop talking to yourself internally.

• Become aware of the sensation of your head resting on your spine. Your spine rises up out of the center of your pelvis. Your pelvis floats freely around the tops of your legs. Separate all of your bones, starting with your toes and moving up your legs, into your pelvis, up your spine, the bones of your rib cage, shoulder girdle, down your arms and fingers, your neck bones, and all the bones that hold your head.

• Sense the space between the soles of your feet and top of your head and the shape of that space. Explore movement that changes and rearranges that space/shape. Feel free to move around the room, and at any speed you want. Enjoy yourself.

• Now, explore movement that rearranges the space/shape between your shoulders and the soles of your feet . . . now your shoulders and your knees . . . your knees and the palms of your hands . . . the palms of your hands and your back . . . your back and your front . . . your shoulders and your pelvic girdle . . . your head and your pelvis . . . your head, your hands and your pelvis . . . your head, your hands, your pelvis and the soles of your feet . . .

• In the next few minutes, connect with someone near you. Focus on the space/shape between you. Improvise movement that rearranges that space/shape.

Space Between expands physical awareness. The exercise is not about conjuring up mental pictures, memories or emotions. This is focused attention on the body, the inside the body, the body in motion and in space. It crowds out the conceptual mind, offers it no room to think.

Most of us, if asked, wouldn't be able to say how our feet are positioned while we brush our teeth in the morning. Nor would we be able to describe the position of our spine as we hand a police officer our driver's license. Even most actors and professional performers, don't track the body.

Space Between searches out the still point that always resides within us. It mutes conceptual activity, an energy that feeds past and future. We do this by bringing our attention into the body. Present time. Now. Our still point is the present; it's the relaxed state where awareness always is. Resting in the still point we brush our teeth, relate to the police officer, dance in our room or perform miracles on stage. Steady. Unswerved by the vast array of stimulation.

Now, we'll listen to space, and shape it, with the sound of "ah." The inside of the mouth will shape "ah" and that "ah" will shape a wave of sound through space.

16B. Chords

• Let's stand in a circle. We'll move around the circle making three pitched chords. I'll begin by making an "ah" sound on a particular pitch, and I'll hold it while the person next to me joins in with an "ah" sound on a different pitch. We'll both hold our tones while the next person, the third, joins with an "ah" on yet a different pitch. The first person ends the chord by gesturing, signalling us to stop. Then, the second person begins the next set. These people must move quickly so that the first person doesn't run out of breath. You can create harmony or cacophony, just be sure to always have three different pitches in each chord.

• Again, let's go around in sets of three. This time I'll tone two "ah" sounds, each on a different pitch, and hold the last. Each person who joins the chord, also, tones two different "ah" pitches and holds his or her last. All six pitches must be different.

• Let's change our timing. We'll return to a single pitch and proceed in staccato fashion. Don't hold your tone. Each "ah" is short, abrupt, and percussive. We'll build up speed as we circle with faster and faster chords. Stay relaxed.

Jonah stands in the circle. His face is paler than usual. He looks so serious. Jonah's terrified. He's never been able to sing, let alone carry a tune. He's been told he's tone deaf. He believes it. His turn is getting closer. Now, it's upon him. He opens his mouth and he hears a scrawny, squeaky, scratchy, vibrating sound that starts and stops, wavers and finally collapses altogether. He tries again. He's sweating and his face is burning. And then again. Finally the person next to him sounds over him and the circle resumes. Nobody's looking at Jonah. Again his turn is getting closer . . .

Many of us come to this exercise with devastating singing experiences from the past, at school, in community organizations, with friends or family. These past events turn our present task into a personal challenge, or a torment. All we can do is notice this experience as clearly as possible and, while holding it, listen. Hear the sounds as they come to us. Our old identifications fade away as interest in the present phenomena we're making together grows. Let the "ahs" grow itself into an amazing event.

16C. Ensemble: Walk/Run/"Ah"

• You'll do a sound and movement ensemble event. Here's how it goes. First, everyone find a place on the floor and stand in relation to one another. In this improvisation, you only have three movement choices: walk, run or stand still. That's all. Nothing fancy. Stay simple.

• Here's where the sound comes in: your movement must always be accompanied with an "ah" sound. The "ah" sound corresponds energetically with the movement and lasts as long as the movement does. They happen simultaneously. So, if you're taking a short relaxed step, the accompanying "ah" sound is the same short duration, and the same relaxed energy.

• You're playing off each other. You will acutely listen and watch each others' sounds and moves. Designing the spatial and choral patterns together. Every sound and every movement you make is relevant to what's already going on.

• Each "ah" sound you make starts and ends the same, on one pitch. But you can make it different. If, for instance, you're walking, each step and breath may be a different pitch.

⌣ •

Some examples of directorial comments:

Stop. Begin again. Too much is going on. Listen more.

Stop. Start over. Too much is going on. This is not the time for you to individually trip off into creativity. Remember, you're in an ensemble.

Stop. Begin again. Make sure you know how the "ah" tones you contribute clearly relate and fit into the whole sound.

Stop. Begin again. Sparsely this time. Allow for silence and stillness.

Stop. Begin again. You can't really have more than two rhythms going on. Not yet. Not until you've mastered listening skills more completely. Then, you'll be able to interweave many different rhythms. If you're "ah-ing" and others come in with a different pattern, either join them, adjust so that the patterns coexist (you should enjoy hearing them together) or stop. Allow yourself to be interrupted. And likewise, if there are patterns going on and you want to introduce a new pattern, know that it will either interrupt what is going on or will coexist with it. Of course, you may wait for an opportune moment, but, by then, you'll probably have a different impulse anyway. Don't hold on to any ideas. They're probably relevant only at the first moment of you have them.

Stop. Begin again. Clarify your spatial patterns. As with the sound, you may have to limit yourself to two or fewer patterns. Of course, those patterns will change. Your collective awareness will determine how many different patterns the improvisation may contain at any moment. You all need to know what the complete action and sound is at all times.

With all these warnings, a student might be afraid to make any kind of move, let alone crash through a safe, secure, neat and orderly improvisation, where everybody's joining, supporting, and listening. Safe, secure, neat and orderly improvisations may or may not cushion challenges, or even catastrophes. But it's always worth a try. Without catastrophes, what was safe, secure, neat, and orderly becomes too safe, secure, neat and orderly and threatens the liveliness of the improvisation.

Of course, the person who brings in a catastrophe (a primary shift of extraordinarily different content that grabs the focus of the scene) must discern the proper moment to make his mark. His action must fall into space with listening. Then, he's free to turn the improvisation around, shift it, stand by his action and relate to the consequences.

～ •

16D. Shift by Interruption

• Get into trios, standing in neutral. This improvisation focuses on a direct relationship between the partners, and will begin once one of you shifts. The shifts may be forms of movement only, sound and movement, speech and movement, sound alone, speech alone, sound and speech together, or speech, movement and sound combined. Whatever expresses your content most appropriately. Develop the shift until one of your partners interrupts with another shift. Each shift should be a response to the previous one. When you're interrupted, freeze your action immediately. Your partner develops their shift until either you or the other partner interrupts, again with a different shift that's a response. Continue to switch back and forth this way, the interruptions coming randomly from any partner at any time.

• The instant you get interrupted, freeze, or pause, and hold that shape until your next shift.

• Each of your shifts will be different, since you always respond to what you interrupt.

• Remember, you're always responding to each other's timing, shaping, use of space, dynamics and content. Use the whole room. You don't need to be confined to the area you're in right now. Particularly focus on the space/shape relation between your body and your partner's.

Direct/Indirect Relationship Again

Remember, when people are improvising in groups (two or more), their relationship may be direct or indirect. In an indirect relationship the partners don't look at each other, or, if they do, it's without recognition. In a sense, they play side-by-side, or parallel. They're aware of each other, and each other's actions, and use that information in their side-by-side play. Their content may be related but doesn't have to be. They're only interacting through the formal (time, space, shape, dynamics) aspects of their actions.

In **Shift by Interruption** relationships are direct. The partners are talking to each other—action-response—as curious and feeling human beings sharing their inner worlds. They look directly at each other when appropriate. They're communicating within the same context, the same story or situation. They're in the same time, space and place. They believe one another's actions are true and real, and respond from their personal resource.

Alternating allows them to experience their separateness and feel their action in relation to the others'. Having the partner stay still while the other is active breaks up the habitual need for concurrent response.

Each action stands alone. The links are temporarily broken.

In direct relationship, what goes on inside of those pauses? Attention stays focused on the partner's actions, alert and receptive to the ongoing events. Feelings may change in response. These feelings lead to the next shift. An audience watching would see the performer's face registering their inner process, whether the performer is listening, thinking, feeling, emoting, spacing out, planning or judging. All this takes place in pause.

When students relate to each other's content directly, their improvisations often become mundane, ordinary, "real-life" like. Content constricts and becomes predictable. The physical relationships become subordinate to the story or emotional interchange between the actors. The improvisation loses its energetic and visual appeal.

Rather than just focusing on the narrow content field, students need to perceive all aspects of current action, the *how* as well as the *what*. In detail. The choral aspects of speech, tones, and rhythms. These improvisations are not to be necessarily realistic. They are to broaden their vision of life, not copy it. Interruptions are important components of the music. Each shift is the next piece of rhythmic interplay between voices and bodies. Students need not be polite. Students don't have to wait for a partner to conclude before they interrupt, but they should always remain curious as to what their partner is up to. They don't blindly cut off their partner as soon as they have an impulse. These interruptions result from a balanced interaction between impulsive curiosity and a sense of music.

We'll take this "**Shift by Interruption**" a step further, widening the possibilities of choice.

16E. 1/3–1/3–1/3

• In trios. Now, you're always active, no longer alternating turns. Proceed through the improvisation by shifting. You're always in the same world/scene and your relationship is direct.

- Whenever you shift, you have three choices. You can:

  1. Introduce new material,

  2. Do what your partner is doing, by joining him or her in form and content,

  3. Be still and silent, in pause.

- Keep a balance between these three choices, generally 1/3 of the total time in each. So, 1/3 of the time you initiate, 1/3 you copy, and 1/3 you're still and silent.

- Whenever you shift, there's some thread in your internal world (subtext) that connects one shift to the next. When you choose to do what your partner is doing, that choice must make sense to you. It must, in some way, fit into your flow of experience. Be clear why you're changing from your action to theirs. Don't pick up their action, just for the sake of it, unless, of course that in itself is the thread.

Dividing your time into these thirds invites balance. It places equal value on the choices of initiating, joining, and pausing. We all have habits that make one of these common to us or more difficult. This forces us to explore what it feels like to do the less accustomed mode.

Subtext

The subtext of an action refers to the thoughts, feelings, or emotion that the performer is experiencing, but

not communicating directly. Subtext may be subtle or blatant. It may even be antithetical to the text. It's all the hidden stuff that we normally bury. An action's meaning is the combined information of the spoken text and the unspoken sub-text.

A skilled performer expresses both the text and the subtext simultaneously. He or she may even be able to express a sub-sub-text, an undercurrent riding beneath both.

For example:

Text: You look wonderful.
Sub-text: She really looks ill.
Sub-sub-text: I wish I could be more honest.

Trios offer dynamic to relationship just by being a threesome. It's not uncommon in 1/3–1/3–1/3 that a partner finds themselves the odd one out. This two-against-one dynamic plays into an archetypal situation: being left out, abandoned, not liked, not good enough, etc. The other two may be in a unified action that ignores the partner, or they may be relating directly to each other, leaving no space for a third party. The odd one out has an opportunity to reorganize their perceptions and responses to a familiar scene. They can choose how they want to play. They don't have to identify with it, since the situation really doesn't have anything to do with them. Or, if it does address them personally, they don't have to buy it.

Here's an example:

John and Camille are reliving an old High School experience. Now, six years later, they're laughing, howling at their innocence. They're recalling friends who played significant roles in the episode. Phil isn't a part of the situation. He can:
   1. Stand quietly and look at them
   2. Stand quietly and look off in the distance
   3. Pace back and forth, indicating his current emotion or indicating nothing
   4. Brush his hair back in slow motion facing the audience
   5. Sit on the floor and rock

6. Intersperse his words with theirs and deliver a text about a different High School experience, or what his politics are, or his love life, or just about anything that comes into his mind

7. Hum

8. Do a soft shoe dance with intermittent pauses

9. Deliver a text placing John and Camille in historical context (reframe)

10. Anything at all

Jumping the Fence

There's a fence one must jump. On one side of the fence is a sense of powerlessness. One can be an object to unrelenting forces, dodging and

darting around them, weakening, even dying. On the other side of the fence is a game, in which one is the subject, the player, free to interpret, redirect, or do nothing with the endlessly changing phenomena. If he remembers the fence, the performer can jump it. He can handle the scene, by taking control of his own destiny. Every improvisational scene is manipulable—it can be changed.

This is not true, of course, in regular theater. An actor might play a character who has been abandoned. The key here is the phenomena of "character." The actor has no personal attachment to the outcome of events. She's not playing herself. When we're improvising, we do play ourselves and often get stuck within our limitations. This practice gives us a broader concept of who we are.

Here's a fence-jumping exercise.

16F. Angels

• Let's sit in a circle. Randomly, with a little space in between, we'll each call out words that describe attitudes or emotions, such as happy, sad, frustrated, pressured, ecstatic. Not physical conditions, just states of mind.

• Now, move off into groups of four. Two of you sit down facing each other. You'll be the actors and have a dialogue, a conversation. The other two, the directors, split up and sit behind them.

• From time to time, the directors will whisper in the ear of their actor a word that describes an attitude or emotion. Directors, do this when your actor isn't talking, when the other actor is talking.

• Actors, when you hear this word, keep it in mind as you listen to the other actor speak. Allow what they say to ignite that emotion or state of mind your director gave you. Then, you respond from that state of mind. Don't say how you're feeling, but be that feeling.

• Avoid speaking in the second person. No "you." Frame your conversation in the first, or third, person. You're not directing your emotions at your partner but speaking from the emotion in the first or third person.

Directors, start your actors off with an emotion.

Emotions, if scrutinized, appear to be a cluster of sensations linked to a cluster of ideas/thoughts. If the focus remains on the ideas/thoughts, then the emotion persists. On the other hand, if the focus rests on only the sensations, then the thoughts vanish with the emotions, since they're intrinsically dependent.

Angels is a body exercise. The director says, "Angry." The actor listens to the other actor, interprets what they're saying so that it will elicit anger and then responds "angrily." They assume "angry's" body and mind. The chest lifts, hand gestures are sharp and forceful, eyes glare, jaw tenses, voice raises volume and pitch, facial skin reddens, language is direct, less metaphoric (as it may be be in "loving," i.e., "Your eyes are like a still pond."), critical, accusing and condemning. Similar body/mind shifts occur with each direction.

Beliefs create reality. We can listen to anything somebody says to us, and, no matter what they're saying, if we want, we'll actually hear reason to support whatever emotion we're carrying. For example:

Judy says "Why don't you come over tomorrow?"

That statement can be heard as a simple invitation. It also can be interpreted as a threat, a sexual advance, manipulation, comfort, support, a busybodys' nosiness, a trap, tease, or talisman.

When we interpret what's being said to us, we project a subtext onto our partner's words. In theater, it's a useful skill to project subtext. Doing so supports the reality we intend to portray. In daily life, it's a different story. We can get ourselves into trouble doing this. Most of the time, we project unconsciously. In **Angels,** we do this consciously. Creating projected subtexts helps us notice how we do this in our lives.

First Person

Students are advised to not talk in the second person, to use the first, or third, person. When we're emotional, we often blame the other for our condition, lashing out, seducing, manipulating, or trying to control them. "You make me feel . . ." " You're being . . . " "Don't you ever . . . " "When you . . . " "You should . . . " "Why don't you . . . " "How about you . . . " In **Angels**, students *use* emotions to prod their imagination and memory. By staying in the first or third person, they must look inward for their world.

> *A Dialogue*
> *Greta: (depressed) I can't seem to leave the house and I'm exhausted. It's been months since I've really even seen anybody, not that there's anybody to see, or anybody who wants to see me, really.*
> *Sam: (peaceful) Staying in the house sounds wonderful. Soup cooking in the kitchen, I can sing a quiet little tune, or read.*
> *Greta: (afraid) Nobody's on the streets anymore. We're all in our little houses. I remember when it was safe. You can't imagine the number of locks I've installed on my doors.*
> *Sam: (angry) I say we lock up everyone who looks suspicious. Impose a curfew. Get them off the crime-ridden streets.*
> *and on and on . . .*

Maybe you've known somebody like this. They constantly misinterpret whatever you say and fly off in a million emotional directions at the slightest provocation. Pretend you're that person.

16G. Performance Score: Disparate Dialogue

• Two people who were partners in the previous exercise (Angels), go out and sit in chairs facing each other.

- Have an Angels-type conversation without a director advising you. You're on your own.

- Listen to your partner. Believe what they say. Respond directly to their content, but from an illogical and emotionally mercurial state of mind. You may interrupt or wait until your partner concludes.

- Remember to listen to the timing, tone and cadence of the language.

Disparate Dialogue explodes the usual confines of conversation. Rather than falling out of themselves and merging into content, this form draws each performer toward his or her own imagination. Each dialogue, while intentionally connected, meanders through fields of information.

The chord toning earlier in the day comes into play. Performers hear one voice follow another. Each turn is a galaxy of sound. Strung together, the sounds are a large chord, with pitches and rhythms. Shapes of sound define spaces of feeling.

Practice

17A. Eyes Closed
17B. Jog Patterns
17C. Space/Shape/Time
17D. Expressive Walk
17E. Mirror Language
17F. Text-Maker and Colorer
17G. Performance Score: Collaborative Monologue

"Practice makes perfect." When we say this, we mean that when we practice a skill, piano playing, for instance, we become more skilled. We get better and better as we aim for perfection. We might, also, say, "Practice makes imperfect." For instance, by habitually not listening, we practice ignorance. Yet, in terms of ignorance, that ignorant practice is ignorant perfect. Perfectly ignorant.

If we practice just to practice with no goal in mind, practice, itself, is what we get better at. Perfect practice. Practice includes both perfection and imperfection, with wide degrees of variation in between and totally new occurrences.

Eyes Closed and Jog Patterns are explorations into the corners of inner and outer attention. They offer infinite rewards. We return to them over and over again, each time picking up where we left off, not with specific images, but with further feelings of ease and safety.

17A. Eyes Closed

• Repeat exercise 5A.

⌣ •

Students are in the fourth week of the training. They're catching on to their tricky mind and its busy-ness. They see how it endlessly fluffs itself, pulling up pictures and stories from the past and musing on the future. They're beginning to disentangle from these pictures and stories, and identify less with their ownership. They're more willing to play with whatever comes up, and this willingness propels them into both gross and subtle moments.

   Their awareness has increased. They notice many details. Curiosity surpasses fear of the unknown. Sensations and feelings connect. Students are in the present. They inhibit themselves less with judgments about their work. Personal identification with changing phenomena is irrelevant. With each new freedom, the body/mind continually rebirths in **Eyes Closed**. Complete experiences cascade upon the consciousness of the mover, endlessly forming and reforming.

⌣ •

17B. Jog Patterns

• Repeat exercise 5B.

⌣ •

The first few times students explore **Jog Patterns**, their patterns are general, generic. For example, they may run back and forth across the space, in circles, or they may split into two groups and move toward and away from each other. Perhaps, they may explore diagonals. Their main concern is not the use of space, so much as keeping track of everyone in the room and refining their communication skills as an ensemble. Now, with more skills under their belt, they're freer to create intricate spatial designs and relationships. They're no longer just bodies in space. The basic form of the jog hasn't changed, but the subtle expressions on their face and shifts of energy and posture indicate the story of the jog.

> *They're all running after each other, round and round. They're trying to catch up to one another. The spirit is playful. One splits off and runs to the corner, then jogs in place. The others notice. Some continue in the circle, but others peel off and race to the corners of the room. Soon, all the corners fill up. A challenge sets up. You can see it in their eyes. Who's going to leave the corner first? The tension builds. Suddenly, they all break out, wildly running in haphazard directions just barely missing each other. Gradually their run cools down, loses steam and they're in a line headed backwards toward the rear wall where they sedately jog, their chests slightly raised, in place, facing the audience . . .*

We'll bring the peculiarities of solitary investigations of **Eyes Closed** into communication/relationship, as **Jog Patterns** did.

⌣ •

17C. Shape/Space/Time

• In partners, do a movement improvisation. Focus on time, space, shape and dynamics. Relate your time patterns, your speeds, when you move and when you don't. Be aware of how you use the space in the room, collectively and individually. Contrast your shapes and energies, at other times be alike.

• We have isolated all of these elements in previous exercises. Now, we are putting them together.

• Be sparing with your movement: concise, precise, conscious. Fill every movement with clear intention, so that your partner understands your intention with a particular movement at a particular time. The movements will have a particularity to them because they're about you. They are your responses to whatever is going on with your partner at that moment. Stay awake.

What's a dream? Isn't it an accumulation of images and stories that erupt from our mind and appear to be real? Don't we believe our dreams while we're in them, while asleep? In the morning, when we wake up, we discover that we were dreaming and that the episodes weren't real after all, but dreams. Sleep is what we think was real. These improvisations are dreams. They're not too different from the dreams we create while we sleep. And, in a sense, not too different from the dreams we create while we're awake. Aren't the day to day perceptions that we create in our minds dreams, too? Aren't we always giving meaning to what has no inherent meaning? Shapes, color, movement, smells. Aren't our interpretations like dreams? So let's make dreams here with time, space, shape, energy and feeling. Let's make stories.

We improvise. Story unfolds. Story is made up from a series of episodes, a chain of actions, causes and effects. There may be a crisis, resolution, question. The events may make sense or they may not, they may be cohesive or not.

Our job is to accept the story as it is, just notice it, and refrain from planning ahead, or writing a script in our minds. Mental work lures our attention from the present and we miss out on the current activity. It's particularly dangerous because our partners can't read out minds. We lose contact with them; they lose contact with us. Then, our actions seem to come from hidden agendas (unexpressed thoughts), and our partners can't understand us.

Because **Space/Shape/Time** is a movement improvisation, dance-trained students tend to relate to the movement through the form, kinetically, and neglect the story. It's important to set an intention for the improvisation before it begins. It's true that in many of the exercises in this training, we isolate and focus on form, but our intention here is to connect through story.

On Day Fifteen, in **Face the Music,** we specifically lived through our face. Let's focus on the face again. Sometimes, the expression on the face and the actions of the body are incongruent. Or, the face doesn't match up with the feeling. Let's practice putting the two together.

﹀ •

17D. Expressive Walk

• Everybody, line up against the back wall and stand side by side with a little breathing room between you. Imagine a narrow corridor in front of you. Walk forward in a moderately slow, neutral pace down your corridor. With each step, change your inner reality, your mind, and change the expression on your face accordingly.

• Remain relaxed. Let your eyes speak as much as the muscles of your face. The tension of your body may slightly change too; stay in your body. Don't change your posture. Don't think of emotions and then act them out. Feel your face, the muscles, movement, and tension of it. Respond to what you sense there. The faces and feelings unfold out of each other. Sensation-Feeling-Action.

• Next step: I'm going to clap, fairly rapidly. On each clap step forward and change your mind/face.

﹀ •

The Face

The face is flesh, it's body. It moves. Feelings find their outward expression through the porous, moveable, flesh of the face. Feelings escape from mental entrapment through the face.

The face shapes itself and feelings follow it. Feeling comes bubbling up to meet the face. The face draws memory and imagination out.

It doesn't matter whether the face calls forth feeling or feeling shows itself on the face. It doesn't matter which happens first. Eventually, there's no first. The face and feeling are unified.

Of course, one may choose to keep their face relaxed, or specifically shaped, and still express feeling. The face isn't the only way to express feeling. The body has motion, breath, the expressions of sound or language work at its command.

If feeling unintentionally stops at the face, the blockage usually comes from fear. We live in fear of being exposed, seen as vulnerable, wrong, out of place, extroverted, rude, romantic, dumb, sweet. Then, tension rises and masks the face with emptiness. The mask may be hardened, or relaxed, with frowns, or smiles. All these masks dull sensibilities. They are a shield against current experience, and they entomb feeling.

Just as a masked face covers feelings, an arbitrarily chosen expression has the potential to call up feeling. For example, right now, smile. Put a big smile on your face and relax. What happens? Doesn't that smile elicit a feeling?

Sometimes, **Expressive Walk** is done in front of a mirror. Students watch themselves and note whether their internal experience matches up with their facial expression. Or they do this face-to-face with a partner and report their observations to each other.

Imagine that language comes from the entire face, not solely from the mouth. Imagine that the face speaks.

17E. Mirror Language

• Sit on the floor, face to face with a partner. One of you speaks, developing a narration. The other mirrors, speaking also. The leader speaks very slowly so the follower can mirror exactly and simultaneously. Slow enough that it's not evident who is leader and who is follower. You're together, exactly.

• Continue until I say switch, and then, right from where you are, change roles. The narration continues with no time lapse.

• It doesn't matter what you talk about. Start with anything. Listen to yourself, believe it. Get involved with it and follow what you hear and feel.

• Be inside each other's mouths, in each other's face.

Expression on the leader's face helps the follower to follow. The leader's slowness helps. So does relaxing. The leader follows their text, the follower follows the leader.

Let's continue on. We'll expand the follower's choices and ease up on the responsibilities of the leader.

17F. Text-Maker and Colorer

• Sit down in trios. You'll collaborate on building a language composition.

• One of you is Text-Maker and the others are Colorers. The Text-Maker provides the language, the narration, story and images. The Colorers can only use the language that the Text-Maker has provided.

• Text-Maker, even though you're providing the language and content of the narration, you're continually listening to your Colorers. Give them room. You may even join them on some little play of words, the three of you riffing together. Don't go on and on, feeling responsible for the whole thing. You are also coloring the language as you speak it. Don't hurry. Take time and give your language play. This exercise is about the three of you co-creating with sound, language and feeling together.

• Colorers, your job is to support, add depth, feeling, atmosphere, and subtextual quality to the text. You can't introduce any new language, no new words. You may only use the words of the Text-Maker. You may, however, change the timing and ordering of phrases and words. You may repeat or retrieve things. You may redesign the expression of the lines as long as you stay within the intention of the Text-Maker. Even if you add other subtextual intonations, don't counter theText-Maker. Your material must always support his or hers.

• Continue until I say stop. After you've stopped, have a little chat about the composition, what you liked or didn't, what worked for you or didn't, what you would like from each other, if anything, and what you can do in your next round to make the composition more of whatever you want. Then, you'll reverse roles.

"I couldn't find room to come in. Your voice was filling up all of the space."

If you think there's no room to come in, come in anyway. Or don't. Relax. "No room" is an idea that blocks your energy and that doesn't feel good. Send your voice out over your partners. Or under. Or mirror. Whatever sounds good. Or bad. Try out bad. That might change things. Always work with what's going on. It's perfect.

"It felt wonderful, as if we were one voice."

Several or many voices can always be heard as one collective voice. The ear expands, sensing, all that it hears as an ongoing stream of sound which becomes single voice. Preferences and judgments create the idea of separation. We usually feel separated from others because we're so involved in our own preferences and judgments, but we could regard everyone's voice as a single stream of voice.

"We repeated too much. I would have liked more new material
to play with."

If repeating is what's going on, take on repeating. Repeat like mad. Enjoy it. Every improvisation is different. This one might be "The Repeating Improvisation."

"I think we can expand our range together. I didn't want to over-
ride you."

Why not? To override someone is an idea. Listen to the sound of the improvisation. What does it want? Fulfill it. Your job is not to protect, or perfect, your partner: thinking of expanding your partner's or the improvisation's range, takes you away from responding to what is going on right then, right there.

Each and every improvisation is happening just as it is. Participants only need to follow the arrows, the cues, the stones that are set down and are continually being placed to reveal it. If participants have the capacity for this to happen, without imposing ideas or preferences from thoughts that have nothing to do with the present moment of experience (sensation), each improvisation will have its own exceptional identity and be unpredictable.

If each improvisation is perfectly what it is, then why bother having discussions afterwards? Because the discussions are for participants to tell each other what they noticed. They describe the elements that molded the improvisation in a particular way. For example, they may notice that a particular improvisation was vocally small, full of whispers and sighs, pauses, even, at times, monotonous, single-toned. By noticing certain aspects, students automatically imply that other characteristics were not present. (If it was this, then it must not have been that.) Pointing out details in an improvisation helps to open up possibilities. Next time, the improvisation may be of greater range. Next time, it might address altogether different aspects.

Now, let's merge the different roles of Text-Maker and Colorer into one role.

17G. Performance Score: Collaborative Monologue

• Two people sit out on the floor, side by side, facing the audience. You both will talk simultaneously and build a monologue together. One of you starts talking, about anything. The other immediately joins in. Listen to each other as you talk so that you can incorporate each others words into your language. You're talking about the same thing at the same time and in the same tone of voice. Your rhythms, inflections, and intonations are the same. Even your body posturing and energy is the same, but you're not mirroring. You're moving too quickly for that, continually talking forward in the monologue while drawing from each other. Don't wait for the other to catch up. You're both talking and retrieving each others' material concurrently. Each of you adds and follows material equally. Maintain a balance between the two. One monologue comes from two mouths.

Collaborative Monologue

This simple and small performance score symbolizes the whole training. In order for it to work, the performers must relinquish all judgments, needs, and preferences. They must not plan anything. They must stay open and receptive to their and their partner's realities equally. They must stay connected to feeling. They're in their bodies. Their energy focus must be free to shift, transform or develop depending on the progression of the improvisation. They must accept and respond immediately with utmost conviction, and without a millisecond's delay, to whatever their partner introduces into the scheme of things.

Merging

From the outside, it looks as if the two performers have merged into one entity even though they're not saying the exact same thing at the exact same time. What's really happening to one is really happening to the other. As individuals, they no longer seem to exist.

Merging often carries with it a negative significance: the individual has become lost, uprooted from her or his centeredness or autonomy, weak and disoriented. But imagine merging two centers, two strengths. When we take two primary colors, yellow and blue, and put them together, we have green. Yellow and blue didn't go anywhere. They spread their molecules out to let each other in. The experience inside of **Collaborative Monologue** is just like that: permeability to the experience of the partner without loss of one's integrity.

Merging isn't agreeing. Agreement implies separation, an "I" and a "you." The "I" must agree with the "you" and the "you" with the "I." We don't even assume agreement with merging. We're free from the constraints and loneliness of that concept altogether.

It's odd to call this Action Theater process a training, or even a practice, since we're not learning anything we don't already know. Actually, we're not learning anything we already aren't. We're remembering and unlearning what stopped us before.

Day Eighteen

Stalk

18A. Four Forms
18B. Elastic Ensemble
18C. Five Feet Around
18D. Levels
18E. Deconstruct Movement, Sound and Language
18F. Performance Score: Collaborative Deconstruction
18G. Performance Score: Threaded Solos

A friend and I were travelling around the Yucatan peninsula in Mexico. One day, we met a man who described a grotto, a cave that held within it several pools of water. The grotto was deep in the jungle about 50 km. south of where we were staying. He told us a local farmer guides visitors into the cave. All of the information was very vague, but, early one morning, we prepared for the adventure. First, we covered ourselves up from head to toe with long pants, long sleeve shirts, hiking boots, neck scarves, rain wear, hats, cotton gloves and sun screen. Then, we packed a compass, a flashlight, extra water, a snakebite kit, antihistamines, and lip balm. This was the tropics and we were going into the jungle; we were explorers, protected from bites, scratches, poisons, too much heat, too much sun, getting lost or thirsty. Intent on beating the heat of midday, we bundled into the car and took off. Fortunately, there aren't a whole lot of roads in the Yucatan, so we didn't have too many choices. After frequent stops for advice, we came to what we thought was the likely area. Two little children were playing in a field. We asked them where we might find

a guide to lead us to the caves. They went to get their father, who was working in a nearby field, and brought him back to us. He told us he was too busy preparing for planting to take us, but that the children could. We must have looked dismayed because before he went back to work, he assured us that they were quite capable. The girl was six and her little brother, four. They were barefoot. She was wearing a little cotton dress and he, nothing but shorts. She had his little hand in hers. Feeling unsure, but not wanting to be insulting, we followed the children across a yard littered with tires, cars and other rusted debris, then behind into the dense foliage that encircled their small house. We followed an overgrown, narrow path, the children skipping along ahead of us, talking, singing, laughing. After a while, we descended a steep hill that dropped right to the portal of the cave. It was a small opening amidst thickly growing vines. Without the children, we never would have noticed it. They led us in. The passageway was dark, a dank, winding tunnel that descended deeper and deeper into the earth. Every so often, the children instructed us to crawl on our bellies to avoid bats hanging overhead. Even then, we sometimes felt them brushing along our backs. A bit further on, following some casual hand signals from the little girl, we skirted around "Pipo," an enormous tarantula, who guarded his little corner of darkness. The children were quite familiar with his idiosyncrasies and even seemed happy to see him. Eventually, we came to the black pools we'd been searching for. Two silent pools, bottomless, clear, rested side by side in a large and dimly lit chamber. We took off our cloths and dove into surprisingly warm and silky water.

Our guides, the little girl and boy, felt as comfortable in the cave as we would feel in our living rooms. They were stalkers, their eyes and ears alerted to any signs of danger, of newness, or change. Their awareness protected them. The jungle, which was so ominous to us, seemed to extend, harmoniously, from their very beings.

To improvise is to stalk. We stalk the objects of awareness, the limitlessness phenomena of sensation, memory and imagination. We dissect this phenomena into details and, through these details, witness our continual experience. At times, these experiences are perilous and, at other times, enlightening. Whatever they are, we greet them openhandedly. Sometimes, this means we have to crawl on our bellies, sliding along, pressed along a wall, even, momentarily disappear. We walk softly, crash into, or fly, whatever helps us greet ourselves.

Unlimited, we'll extract and explore four possibilities from a vast range.

18A. Four Forms

• Everyone, distance yourself from one another and stand with your arms relaxed by your sides. I'll describe four forms, or activities, to you. For the next ten minutes or so, improvise by switching back and forth between them. Spend as long as you like in each one. Don't rush through. Be sure to keep the forms distinct from one another. In other words, don't blend or merge their aspects. Shift clearly from one to another.

• In the first form, involve yourself with only breath. No movement. Remain still in whatever posture you're in. Play with the ordering, rhythm, depth, and force of your breath. No voice, just breath.

• The second form is very slow and continuous movement in silence. No sounds, stops, starts or pauses. Ever moving slow-motion.

• The third is large, loud, travelling, sound and movement. Keep the sound and movement linked and always travel through the room with it.

• The final form is non-stop talking. Stop moving for this one, be completely still and put all your attention into your talking. Let one idea lead you to the next, free associate, lose control. Play with these forms a while.

• Sometime in the next few minutes, associate with someone near you. Form a partnership and continue improvising within these four forms. Now, you're in direct relation with each other; you're in the same world. Every move, every shift is a response to your partner and is either in the same form, or one that's different.

These four forms were chosen for their contrasting qualities. Others could also work, since it's contrasting quality that's pertinent to the exercise.

If students are able to find reason to shift from silent, slow-motion movement to loud sound and movement, then, they can find reason to shift from anything to everything. The shift must reflect an internal logic.

In other words, it must make sense to them. The process must be a living experience.

Why would one want to shift from very slow movement to loud, boisterous, sound and movement? What inspires someone to shift from a non-verbal orientation to language? Well, we're forcing an issue here, but we're exercising the mind. The mind is a limb of the body. Take an arm, for instance. If the arm doesn't move for an extended period of time, it atrophies, withers, loses its capability for movement, and forgets. Then, it has to be coaxed back, reminded, exercised, and encouraged to recover.

If intention is there, the mind can expand to accommodate and rationalize any contrasting realities, no matter how quickly they arise and how unreasonable they initially appear. Imagination doesn't attach itself to anything. It doesn't want to stay put or not stay put. It's just out of practice. Now, we crawl on our bellies, avoiding the bats. Now, we pay homage to the tarantula. Now, dive into the luxury of the pool. If we can adapt to external changes, we can adapt to internal ones. We are stalking change, adapting adapting itself.

All of this inner stalking, tripping off into the imagination, can distract us from the world around us. The latter part of the exercise moves the student into a partnering relationship, and insists that they come out of themselves enough to notice the other, empathize and share reality-making.

Limited to four choices, participants engage with the forms differently each time they return to them. Since one form is slow with no voice; another largely physical and vocal; another, only breath with restrained body; and the fourth, pure language, each addresses a different quality of energy and brings contrast and liveliness to communication. Each form, centers on particular aspects of the mind (slow moving = sadness, sensuality; large sound and movement = joy, or maybe, rage). Slow movement might mean something different the second time around, or the fourth, or fifth. Any form can be the voice of just about anything.

Language Forms

We have many ways to structure language interaction. How we structure the interaction affects the content. Some of these are as follows:

Simultaneous Monologues: Two or more speakers intersticing language with no bridge of content. They're in a musical relationship, exploring time, pitch, rhythm, volume, and tension.

Collaborative Monologue: Two or more speakers simultaneously offering language and using each other's language to form a single monologue.

Merging Monologue: Two or more speakers beginning with simultaneous monologues, then gradually taking on each other's content until all monologues become one.

Text-Maker/Colorer: Two or more speakers: one provides the language: repeating words, changing sound and/or playing with their syntax; the others may repeat words, change their sound and play with their order, but they cannot introduce new material. Both the Text-Maker and the Colorer are collaborating on the total sound expression.

Dialogue: Two or more speakers exchanging language in direct relationship.

Dialogue/Monologue: Two or more speakers alternating between dialogue and monologue modes, stepping in and out of the content of each.

Text-Maker/Echoer: Two or more speakers. One provides the language; the others enhance what the speaker says by using the language provided. They may only repeat words in the order they hear them and as they hear them. Both the Text Maker and the Echoer collaborate on the total sound expression. (See bulking)

Co-Creative Monologue: Two or more speakers alternate speaking and following the same content; they take turns developing the same story.

The following exercises further explore aspects of awareness, relationship to others, and space.

18B. Elastic Ensemble

• Form trios. You'll be doing a movement improvisation and your focus will be on space.

• Imagine that the entire surface of your body is connected by elastic bands to the entire surface of each of your partner's bodies. Every movement that any one of you makes, reverberates and causes reciprocal movement in the two partners. Each reciprocal movement corresponds in energy to the initial movement. If the distance between you is short, then the reciprocal movements would be of very similar energy; if the distance is great, then the reciprocal movements would diminish in energy relative to the distance.

And ...

18C. Five Feet Around

• Everybody, spread out on the floor. Make sure you have five feet of empty space around you on all sides.

• Here's the game. Two rules: 1) you want to get close to everybody else, right up next to them; 2) you can't allow anyone to get closer to you than five feet. It's contradictory, but don't analyze, just play.

And ...

18D. Levels

• In trios. Do a movement improvisation. The three of you are always in the same world. Your relationship is direct. One of you must always be occupying one of these three levels: lowest level (prone on the floor), mid-level (kneeling or sitting), highest level (upright). If one of you changes level the others must adapt. Remember each level must always be occupied.

These are stalking exercises. Both seem to require eyes in the back of your head and the alertness that's present in sports, or when one is in danger.

When improvising with partners, you don't want to miss a trick, not a single gesture, word or expression. Even a subtle change of presence could indicate a shift in the scene, a challenge or a threat.

We exist in a center of space. Everyone occupies their own center. There's space all around each and every one of us. Too often, we only relate to the space in front of us. True, we can't see what's behind us, but we can develop the ability to sense what's going on back there by listening with our ears and our bodies. We can sense someone close behind us, or when we're being looked at, or when someone enters the room. Much, much more is possible.

As with **Pusher/Comeback** in Day Ten, assertiveness and receptivity are key factors in both of these games. One player catapults themselves toward another and dislocates them, makes them move away. Feelings of aggression, passivity, empowerment and disempowerment may surface. The bullies rise to the occasion and so do the meek. Memories and opinions relative to athletics may return for another haunt. These exercises provide a fresh look at old stories. Hopefully, students are ready to discard identifications packed onto these actions, leaving the actions bare to be moving energies, free for everyone's use; free for alls.

This is the eighteenth day of the training and, yet, we seem to be exploring very basic material. We could explore basic material on the eighteen-thousandth day of the training. Even then, it would be possible to take a fresh look at moments of experience. We, the perceivers, are organisms in flux, always changing. How we approach a ceremony, read a book, respond to a question is unknown. At this point of the training, students approach these tasks supported by accumulating wisdom. They would relate to these games very differently if they were presented during the first week.

The following exercise, in its simplicity, demands patience, control, keen observation, and musical orientation. Students are now prepared.

18E. Deconstruct Movement, Sound, Language

• In partners. Partner A, assign to partner B a simple, repeatable movement or gesture. Partner B, practice this movement several times until it is familiar and you understand how it is organized, the parts that make it up.

• As partner A watches, partner B deconstructs the movement: she breaks down the whole movement into smaller parts without changing the form. The bones of the movement stay the same. She does one part at a time, and, then, re-orders the parts, switching back and forth among them, increasingly incremental, increasingly smaller bits of action. Play with the timing inside of each action. Notice the minute details of the action and play with each one of those details. New ones will continually appear. Don't limit yourself.

• B, connect to every moment, be each action, feel it. You may slow actions down or speed them up. But be careful not to change the original form. A, if you notice B changing the form, the skeleton, call that to his attention so he can return to the original form and continue on.

• Each action is a tiny shift. Just as you created an inner logic in Four Forms, do the same here. These abrupt little movements are a living experience for you. You're feeling engaged, moment-to-moment.

• Switch roles.

• Now, partner A gives partner B a sound and movement action, where the sound and movement are linked. This time, B will deconstruct both the sound and the movement, either simultaneously or separately. You can even reorder things. The sound and the movement may no longer be linked as they were in the original form, but may be recombined in different ways.

• Switch roles.

• Next, partner A gives partner B a language phrase and gesture. B, deconstruct the phrase as you have just done with sound and movement. Take apart the words and movements, divide them up into pieces. Re-order those pieces. Sometimes the pieces are minute, sometimes large. Surprise yourself. Don't plan. Listen and let what you hear lead you on to your next action, to your next feeling.

• Switch roles.

Deconstruction

Each one of these exercises asks for deconstruction, and then, reconstruction of the deconstructed material. Students break apart action, dissect simple behavior that slips by unnoticed. They come up with bits and fragments of abstract experience which they have to make into a new sense.

Everything, all that we do, say, see and hear, whirs past us. It's as if we're always squinting, seeing our world diminished, in outline. If we stalk, slow down, empty out all ideas about content, then we notice worlds among worlds of phenomena, details upon details. Even moving your hand is a complex choreography, some of which isn't visible, but only felt.

Begin to wave your hand. Only begin. The very, very beginning.
Just a bit of tension fills the arm, preparing to lift it.

Wave your arm. Where are you waving from? Your wrist, or your shoulder, or both? Probably some of both? Do your fingers bend at the joints or stay fixed? Is your torso moving sympathetically. Your head? Eyes?

If you're waving your right hand from side to side, does your thumb move towards and away from the other fingers on each direction?

Deconstructing a hand wave, you can see how many aspects there'd be, yet we've hardly begun our research. The in-between places, the beginnings of things, the parts that are thrown away, the minor players, the fillers, transitions, mistakes, cuts, slips of the tongue, everything that we devalue or overlook has treasures for the brave and patient.

We're not simply unearthing, analyzing and reconstructing phenomena. We're *feeling* our way through, connecting to each moment of discovery with feeling and passion, dancing and voicing with engaged awareness: finding ourselves and becoming what we find.

18F. Performance Score: Collaborative Deconstruction

• Four people get up and stand, side by side, in front of the audience. Four others go up and, each of you, give a language phrase accompanied with a gesture to a different one of them, and return to join the audience. Keep the gestures and language short and simple.

• The four performers begin by repeating the entire phrase and gesture, one or two times, in relation to what you sense from each other. Then, begin to deconstruct your action.

• The four of you will improvise together and collaborate, playing with your deconstructions. Don't look at each other. You're facing the audience. Listen to each other. Sense each other, stay connected. Blend, weave, interlace, chorus, punctuate, back-up, be similar, contrast, feel your music together.

Collaborative Deconstruction

• After some time, I'll give you a two-minute cue. Within that time, find an ending.

Remember the braids mentioned earlier? Action Theater training braids themes, each time drawing out more details. We braid themes such as relaxing, listening, feeling, timing, music, shape, space, and dynamics. We weave them into tighter and tidier relationships.

Collaborative Deconstruction calls for precise imprints of movements and sounds, fierce listening and unhesitant responses, eyes on all sides of the head, one collective ear, a unified dance from a four-fold body, and a unified chorus from a four-fold voice. Through content-less grunts, whinnies, groans, twitches, thrusts and snaps, four humans experience themselves as one animal.

So far, every exercise on this day has been tightly programmed, with narrow limits set in place before the improvisations began. Now, we open the windows and doors, breathe, and, without constraints, follow our hunches.

⌣ •

18G. Performance Score: Threaded Solos

• It's time for solos. Sitting in a line, we'll start at one end and move on down from one person to the next. You can choose to improvise for 1, 2, or 3 minutes. We'll pass a watch and you'll be timed by the person that precedes you. When your time is up, they'll call out, "Time," loud and clear.

• Thread your solo to the one before it. Take something, some aspect, and use it as a base from which you take off. It may be a sound, movement, phrase, feeling, association, whatever comes to mind.

• Someone from the audience, give the first person an action to start them off.

• We won't stop and discuss these works. We'll just move from one to the next, making a continuous chain of related matter.

⌣ •

Pulling a thread from the preceding solo stops the watching performers from planning their improvisation ahead of time. They can relax, forget themselves, and simply be with one another.

Watching each other perform is not too different from watching one's self. As is frequently the case, a person who is highly judgmental and always analyzing others' actions with a critical perspective, turns the same process onto herself. She analyzes, evaluates, and judges, withholding herself from participating in her own experience. Being part of an audience, is an opportunity to relax, accept, and empathize.

Sitting in the audience also mirrors performing. It mirrors sitting on a bus. Each experience is an opportunity to relax and receive, by sensing what's happening.

> *Greta sees Pola struggling within her solo. Greta's mind takes over. Pola should do this or that, thinks Greta. Pola should confess her struggle. Pola should use third person. Pola should relax her arms. Pola should listen to herself. Pola should just pause for a minute and collect herself. Pola should breathe. Where's Greta?*

If Greta were struggling within her own solo, she would most likely go through the same process. Instead of going into the struggle, she'd involve herself with distracting and correcting devices all the time, running further and further away from herself.

Suppose, as Greta watched Pola, she became the experience she was watching and felt it from inside herself. After the improvisation ended, Greta could describe her experience while watching Pola, without the risk of personal projection, or agenda, interfering with her evaluation.

Stalking may be seen as tracking, following, pursuing, going after something we don't have. We need not limit our concept of stalking to this vein. Stalking is relaxing, slowing down, noticing, being alert. Stalking is experiencing phenomena directly, no separation between the stalker and what is being stalked. To stalk is to be. Diffused of emotion, it is no more or no less than heightened awareness.

Day Nineteen

People and Props

19A. No Pillows
19B. Body Parts/Shifts
19C. Beginnings
19D. Props
19E. Simultaneous Solos with Props
19F. Performance Score: People and Props

Schtick

The Yiddish word shtick *originally referred to a comedy bit or a particular talent. Now the word is used as a derogatory comment referring to patterned or habitual behavior that exhibits itself over and over again.*

It's likely that most shticks *originated as spontaneous actions. Subsequently, because of positive reinforcement, they became set as permanent fixtures of behavior. As long as the audience isn't familiar with the performer, the* shtick *works. Then again, because some audiences crave the familiar, many performers have built careers of* shticks.

We're improvising. That means we're proceeding through experience in a moment-to-moment way. But, *shticks* do come up and when they do, our job is to investigate and follow their details. We can only do that if we recognize the *shtick* as an empty action of habit, devoid of any value right now. If we can do that, we're already past the *shtick*, outside, beyond and through it. Our *shtick* becomes a memory.

To truly improvise, one must be willing to fall or fly off the psycho/physical edge that separates familiar experience from the unpredictable. One must be willing to go where the terrain is fresh, unusual, and even strange.

In these moment-to-moment explorations, there's no *shtick*. There's no familiar or unfamiliar. There are no edges between things. Instead we experience unrelenting change of energy, rhythm, sound, shape, motion, language, and feeling.

We'll begin as an ensemble.

⌣ •

19A. No Pillows

• Everyone, place yourself somewhere on the floor and stand in a neutral posture.

• Some of you will be Sounders and some of your will be Movers. When you're a Mover, you're silent and when you're a Sounder, you're still. Everyone is collaborating, the Movers with one another, the Sounders with other Sounders, and the Movers and Sounders with each other. You are collaborating on how you design the space in the room with shapes, clusters, lines. You will collaborate on time patterns, whether you're moving or sounding. You're collaborating on the development of the content. Everything relates to everything else and you're always in the scene together.

• You can shift the two roles of Sounder and Mover at any time. If you're moving and you decide to become a Sounder, don't return to neutral. Instead, sound from a posture and location that's relevant to that moment. Movement leads to sound and sound leads to movement. There need be no gaps.

• After twenty minutes or so, I'll give you a two-minute cue. Within that time, find an ending together.

⌣ •

Everyone stands still. A low hum arises. It goes on for a long time. Within it, ethereal shadings and harmonies appear. The hum stops. There's a pause. Someone walks to the wall. Another a pause. Someone sways and falls to the floor. Someone else walks to the wall and delicately touches it. The hum, fuller now, resumes, and, out of the hum, a single wail emerges and then gradually it is joined by a myriad of echoes, wailing, wailing. More people fall, roll, get up, go to the wall or fall again. The wail continues on, now dragging its own rhythm. They become silent and in silence the wailers sway and lunge. Then they wail on. Another pause. Everything stops. Some moments go by. Tension mounts. Suddenly a small band of hunched-over people scurry back and forth taking small and light, spritely steps. They huddle together and move as if their bodies are joined. Occasionally one stretches up, spreads his fingers, face and mouth wide open, then becomes still voicing sharp and cutting, high-pitched sounds. Everyone else is moving extraordinarily slowly, sliding their hands over themselves, and each other . . .

Students move from Sounder to Mover with flexibility and speed. They express actions comprised of both sound and movement, intricately intermeshed units. Everyone is both sounder and mover all the time. They pause in one role in order to execute the other, but still hold both roles inside. A continuous line of listening runs underneath the sounds and movements connecting them in time and content.

The ensemble builds a dream-like event. No one could possible explain what it's about. Yet, they seem to understand, and resonate with the content as it unfolds. The images of the participants may be archetypal, symbolic, and seem to refer to an ancient intelligence. Or they may be silly or mundane. Whatever the nature of the actions are, they come from a heightened awareness. The form's peculiar demands insist on it.

Imagination is an expanded perception of reality accessible through skills.

Skills are needed to use tools.
The voice, the body, and language are all tools.

If our voice can cover many octaves, and we have control over our breath, we have more options to investigate, combine, and transform. If our mind is always aware of our body, we will experience more possibilities to recast, redirect, and reorganize physical experience and movements. We train ourselves to hear the sound of our speech and sense language shaping inside our mouths. Thus, we can hear ourselves from the outside.

Once we really listen to ourselves, we can become aware of our habitual shticks: what they are, where they are, when they show up. If we tune into the inside moments of each word, we won't be blinded by our schticks. Once we tune in, we can play.

Let's retool body awareness.

19B. Body Parts/Shifts

• Everyone, find a place on the floor and stand in a neutral posture.

• We're going to practice shifts, but with a little twist. I'm going to call out different parts of your body. When you hear the first body part, begin a series of shifts with that body part being the central physical focus of each shift. As you hear each subsequent cue, change focus so that your next series of shifts is physically centered on the next body part.

• Have your shifts alternate between:
   movement,
   sound and movement,
   sound only,
   language and movement and
   language only.

• If you're sounding, or talking, from stillness, continue to focus upon the appropriate body part.

• Relax. Take time to totally involve yourself with each moment of experience.

Do this. Twist your head down and to the right as far as you can. The rest of your body remains limp. Continue putting energy into the twisting action. Sound from there. Stop. Change your mind and talk from there. Stay with the twisting energy. Stop. Sound from there again. And again talk. Let the twisting energy effect your voice and your feelings. What does that voice, those feelings have to say?

Wobble your knees and walk. Wobble and walk. Wobble and walk. You're a wobbly knee walker. Believe it. How does this make you feel? Continue to pay detailed attention to the wobbles, every one of them, and the walk, every step. Change your mind. Sound. Stop. Talk.

Hold up your right hand. Rotate it extremely slowly to the right and then to the left. As slowly as you can. Look straight ahead. What mood does that action put you in? Talk. Stop. Change your mind. Talk again.

This exercise leads to the experiencing of language as a felt action cradled by the body. We discover that we always talk with our body while we use language, whether consciously or unconsciously. Becoming conscious of the body's dynamics within the voice widens our options. The body and language simultaneously offer complementary, or juxtaposing, aspects to the completed image that speaks personally from the performer's idiosyncratic perceptions.

Slow Starts

Often improvisations get off to a slow start. Fidgets, glances, shifting weight from foot to foot predominate. A slow start can be the manifestation of an unwillingness to dive in, assert oneself, or be clear and forthright about whatever is going on at the time. If the imagination isn't actively illiciting images, there are other things going on. Something always is. The breath, for instance, or current feelings, emotions or thoughts. Fidgets can be excellent choices to start off with if the performer is dedicated and committed to their presence.

The mind and body are rarely quiet. If they are, that's certainly a fine place to begin, too.

We're going to practice beginnings.

19C. Beginnings

• Everyone, partner up. You'll do a series of one minute solos. Switch back and forth. Time each other. Give each other a word cue before each solo. The words can refer to form or content, for example, fast time, blood, blind, blonde, sharp, soft, crescendo, stop/go, Mississippi, etc.

• Have each solo be a mix of movement, sounds and language.

• Dive in. Start strong.

Strong doesn't necessarily mean big or forceful. It means committed. Whatever the impulse is, fill it up to the very top. Feel it. Sense all of its parts. Care for your action as you would a newborn, with fierce, protective love.

Any action, thoroughly sensed and felt, lifts out of and beyond ordinariness. It carves through space and time, leaves no shadow of doubt, and needs nothing in front of or behind it to verify its existence. A sensed and felt action is complete.

Handling objects is another pathway into presence.

19D. Props

• Everyone, take the objects that you have brought with you today and spread them around on the floor. Sit next to one object and without touching it, sense it. Climb inside of the object, become it, and sense what that experience would be like.

• Now, everyone, sit next to another object, one that someone else brought and step inside of it. Now another. And another. Leave your objects where they are and come off the floor.

• One person at a time, go out onto the floor and pick up an object, any object you're drawn to, not necessarily the one you brought. Interact with it. Open up your perception to free the object of its common definition, its usual role or function. For example, if you've chosen the object we call "broom," disidentify it. Strip it of its name and function. Sense its aspects, shape, weight, density, color, texture, smell, etc. Play with it as a nameless phenomenon. Move with it. Explore other functions. Let the object become your partner; perhaps it will lead and you will follow.

• When five or so minutes are up, put it back down on the floor and return to the audience. After you've watched for awhile, you can go back onto the floor to explore another object.

• It may happen that more than one of you is on the floor at the same time. Make room for this. Be aware of each other's physical presence.

◣ •

With props, students practice noticing physical properties, and from that rawest of material (shape, color, weight, movement, texture) create worlds.

Perceptions trigger the imagination, thereby producing identities and function. They notice and explore the physical aspects of the partner-object. Props become partners, partners with no inherent personality, or function, that has to be figured out or accommodated. The performer lays to rest the psychological or relational issues, which come along with living partners. They create the identity and function of their partner-object and have the power to change it at any time.

Use props that are fairly generic and can sustain two or three different readings.

A sample of props:

Roll of butcher paper
Red umbrella
Square white floor fan
Length of heavy rope
Ten-foot tubular pillow
Tree pruner
Colored silk scarves
Bucket of cow bones
Rusted wheel
Stack of books
Green garden hose
Pack of pink file cards

Jess wraps himself with the hose tighter and tighter, constricting his flesh. Judy runs snapping the tree pruner in front of her. Flor lines up rows of books and then tenderly walks on them. Tony sits upright on the rusted wheel and spins himself very slowly, eyes rolling. Tanya wraps her head and face in a red scarf and calls out, her mouth opening and closing. Pete snaps the file cards like karate chops onto the floor. Terri conducts an argumentative dialogue with the rope. Sabine struts elegantly across the back wall, holding the fan out in front of her. Sam rolls around on the butcher paper, crunching and tearing at it. Stephan makes a very tidy bed of bones and then lays down on them.

We live in a world of form. We're surrounded by masses of shapes, colors, textures and movements. It's a rare occasion when we take a moment from our day-to-day business to see what's around us. A trip to the museum, a day in the country, but even then we often see form as content. Tree as "tree" is a static experience. Sensing the phenomenon that we call tree, without naming it, sets up a present time and open-ended interaction.

Working with objects offer students relief. Objects implore, "Touch me, move me, move with me," drawing the performer toward them and into the realm of image and material, sensation and vision. The burden of having to make something happen lifts. Once handled, felt, seen, moved, and moved with, objects lose their conventional boundaries and burrow into the imagination. The object reduces the pressure on the self as subject.

We played with objects as children. We were adept at making imaginary worlds with them. As adults, we're not very far away from that particular grace. It's familiar, but we don't allow ourselves to do it. We've forgotten why this is pleasurable, why we did it.

Sylvia was improvising with two chairs. She put them down and began to talk to them as if they were her parents. Later on in the improvisation, she sat on one of the chairs. It was as if she sat on her mom.

As soon as the performer addresses an object (Sylvia's chair), it becomes permanently fixed in that space. The performer's acknowledgements fill it with life. Objects, whether real or imaginary, or characters or entities, are integral aspects of the scene. Unless the performer initially indicates their temporality (i.e. "Jim, you're only there now, aren't you?"), the object can't be forgotten or ignored.

The same holds true with an alluded to object that's not physically present. Suppose Roberta talks to an imaginary baby in her improvisation, holds it for a period of time and then puts it down on the floor. Whether she's relating to that baby or not, the baby remains for us in that space on the floor unless she directly indicates that it's gone. In fact, if she were to inadvertently step on that spot, we would so strongly hold the baby in our mind there, that to us, she would be stepping on the baby.

19E. Simultaneous Solos with Props

• Three people, choose a prop and go out onto the floor. You'll each improvise, alone with your prop, at the same time.

• Here's how it goes. Develop your own content, separate and different from the others. Create a formal link between yourselves. Share and co-create both the physical and the sound space. Be aware of what your partners are doing, how they are doing it, and how what you're doing formally relates to their activity. Your timing and movement through space, the spatial level you're on, the shapes you're making and the energy you're working with, all relate to your partners.

• Start simply. Only fill the space with the quantity of activity that you can hold in your collective awareness. Remember to keep your content separate from other peoples'. Don't draw from each others' images. Don't even look at each other directly. Use peripheral vision and hearing instead. Hold the entire event in your mind.

• At some point I'll say, "Two minutes." Within that time, end.

Students are collaborating on visual landscapes. They're focusing their exploration on the physical, energetic and temporal components of theater. Eliminating direct relationship from their interaction simplifies the exploration.

Merging Content

For some, it's not hard to maintain separate content while interacting formally. For others, it is. We're accustomed to merging content. I say, "Hello." You say, "Hello," back. I say, "How ya doin'?" You say, "Fine." We don't know how to be with someone and not be affected, or reactive, to their mental and emotional expressions.

Props help to break this habit. The performers' primary relationship is with their prop. They're aware of everyone else's activity, but they're not merging content with anyone else's. Their world is their prop. Somebody running around the room with a big red ball yelling, "Fire," would affect them, but the stories would remain independent and different.

The audience experiences these separate stories and images as a composite, a whole event. They find conceptual and physical connections between snippets of content and between the separate stories. It's to the performer's advantage to know what the audience knows, and see what the audience sees. After all, the performers are in charge. It's their show. Their intention is to communicate what they want. They may choose to allow chance happenings to go without a response, but there's no reason why they should miss out on enjoying (and responding to) them as much as the audience does.

> *John slams a ladder onto the ground. Without missing a beat, Gert starts to sing a be-bop kind of song.*

It's as if the ladder, upon hitting the floor, caused a chain reaction of displaced molecules, setting in motion Gert's song. John and Gert fill the room with a dynamic interplay of actions and responses while remaining in separate worlds.

19F. Performance Score: People and Props

• Again, three people choose different props and go out onto the floor, together.

• You're in the same world sharing both content and forms. You're in a direct relationship with your partners. The props are integral aspects of your collaborative world.

• You're not limited to the prop you started with. All the props are fair game for everyone. They can change hands and change meaning.

• In a sense, there are six of you out there: three animate, three inanimate.

Props may be used as metaphors for internal states. For example, the way one carries a big red ball, lightly on the tips of fingers, or violently clutching the ball to the body, can indicate very different responses to the exclamation, "Fire!" Calmly sifting little mounds of dirt, or frantically wrapping oneself in plastic, while saying, "Fire," would indicate two very different subtexts. The subtleties of handling an object can speak beyond language, beyond sound and beyond free movement. The gestalt of how I speak and move creates a particular meaning at any given moment.

Three people plus three props equals six elements. The combination of the six create a unity of motion, image and energy. Unity always exists. Whatever's on the stage, or in the living room, is a whole, an entirety, consciously designed or not. The performer benefits from connecting with that wholeness, and experiencing themselves and their partners within it as well. They benefit by knowing their world.

In these prop exercises, ordinary objects are perceived as empty forms. They are defined beyond normal summarization, utility or function. To believe an object has only one meaning, is to believe from habit. The familiar, the *shtick*, restrains one's imagination. Habits need to be left behind here. The *shtick* disappears. As each improvisation proceeds, objects are named and renamed, acquiring new functions. Imagination rubs up against the senses, defining and redefining the material world.

Dream On

20A. Walk/Sound, Solo/Ensemble
20B. Superscore
20C. Performance Score: Dreams

We've spent the last nineteen days developing skills of expression and expanding awareness. We've taken apart behavior, looked at its aspects and consciously reformed our actions. We've focused on detail. We've exercised and exercised and memorized a lot of rules and agreed on many conventions. In the end, after all the considerations, thoughts, insights and analysis, it's the body that does the job; if it's listened to and trusted, it will know what to do with surety.

20A. Walk/Sound, Solo, Ensemble

• Go somewhere on the floor and stand in a neutral posture. Breathe. Quiet your mind and relax into your body.

• You have three choices: walk, sound or pause. When you're walking, keep your walk simple and functional. When you're walking, you're not sounding, and when you're sounding, you're not walking. In other words, you're sounding from stillness and walking in silence. These are separate actions.

• Practice this on your own until it becomes comfortable. Let the voice and the movement interact and rhythmically alternate in irregular patterns. Both the voice and the walk will express your story, feelings, subtext, etc.

- After a while, I'll say stop. Everyone return to neutral. Keeping within the same form of sounding and walking as separate actions, build an ensemble piece.

- You're collaborating on three levels: the sound, patterns of travel, and content of the scenes.

- At some point, I'll give you a two-minute cue to end.

A simple score such as this one, like so many others in the training, can be played over and over again. Each time will be entirely different from the others. In this exercise, **Walk/Sound, Solo/Ensemble**, the physical action is limited to a walk, but the collective choreography can become quite complex. There's infinite opportunities for variation in the timing and spacing of each step. Combined with the choral overlay and the unfolding chain of events, walking leads to a full-bodied and multi-dimensional improvisation. As mentioned earlier, separating vocal actions from physical actions demands control, focus, and an acute body awareness. By now students have acquired these skills. Within the context of this exercise, their actions appear ritualized, formal.

We don't usually separate the vocal from the physical elements of our actions. When we do, our behavior appears peculiar. What's peculiar is that the form is highlighted. We're noticing it more than we usually do. A balance between the form and the content seems odd because most of the time we pay attention to the content.

Ritual and Ceremony

As soon as we focus on the formal elements, the details of how an act is executed, we're in ritual. In this sense, in Action Theater, we always create ritual or ceremony because we always balance form and content.

Rituals and ceremonies don't stress the individuality of the person. The act is the focus, not the person performing the act. The act is what *must* be performed, over and over again. In these exercises, instead of focusing only on the action, we focus on the person simultaneously. This brings both the person and the form into the foreground.

Our lives are full of ceremonies: taking the sacrament, lighting the Sabbath candles, exchanging wedding vows, cutting the birthday cake, blowing out candles, singing together, singing the national anthem, greeting each other, washing dishes, fixing the morning coffee.

Often actions are motivated by personal agenda that clouds perception and puts the content up front. The next time you pick up a cup of coffee, let the form take over. Feel how the cup moves through space. Give that form as much attention as the need to bring the coffee to your lips.

Ensemble Awareness

If an ensemble has been practicing together for some time, honing their collective awareness, individuals can begin to assert their identity in more impacting ways. In the early stages of ensemble practice, everybody concedes to, and joins in on, the collective actions. Large groups may be joining to relate to other large or smaller groups, but rarely does an individual stand apart. The fear is that too many individuals will stand apart, splintering the ensemble and dispersing attention. At some point, and with practice, an ensemble can hold a solo, duet or trio, because everybody is tuned in to it. Everybody knows what's going on. They offer supportive action, allowing the primary event to develop.

For example, suppose the entire ensemble is lined up against the back wall facing the audience and making wild gyrations and sounds. Cassie steps out and walks directly forward toward the audience as if in a trance, teetering and moving her mouth and hands soundlessly.

Some examples of supportive ensemble action to Cassie's action may be:

Downplaying or fading,
Becoming still,
Offering vocal backup,
Offering movement backup,

Shadowing or echoing her action,
Becoming other objects that fit into her world.

An ensemble improvisation can be a continuous exchange of primary (Cassie) and secondary (supportive) players, no matter how many performers.

Imagining Beyond

Solo and duets risk ensemble fracturing and eruption of archetypal dynamics: us-against-them, competition, antagonism, and out-right warfare. How do we avoid this? Or better yet, what can we do when this arises? If everyone in the ensemble remains conscious of their actions—responsible for their words and deeds, focused on the moment-to-moment aspects of their actions, disentangled from personal identifications—when warfare-like action of any kind happens, it will be imaginatively enacted without reference to already known concepts or opinions. A sharply pointed finger will be experienced as a shape in space, the turn of a back as a dance, the fall from an attack as a contour of time and movement. The performer looks at the roles of aggressor and victim as a composite of feelings, movements, and voices. Rather than a stereotyped diminishment of these situations, perception expands into enlightened experience.

Whether working as an ensemble, small group, or individual, performers experience the challenge of staying with an image, an action, a feeling, or a quality of being, for an extended period of time. We've all experienced the urgency to move on and see what's next, to get involved in more activity. We're impatient, restless, judgmental; we're afraid of taking up too much space, afraid of not taking up enough.

The more practiced one is, the more drawn one is to step out, away from the crowd and to stay there for however long it takes. The more relaxed and practiced one is, the more one is capable of, and enchanted with, less activity. Simple moments take on awesome relevance and inconsequential events become enrapturing.

The following score pulls together all of the skills accumulated throughout the month.

20B. Superscore

• In trios. Find a place on the floor and stand neutral in relation to your partners.

• The Superscore is the master score, an open improvisation without a particular focus. Everything you've studied, explored, understood, tooled up, and gained insight into comes into play here. Here's a list of reminders:

> • Move, sound or speak in any combination or separately.
>
> • Shift, transform or develop your forms.
>
> • Join each other or do something different.
>
> • You and your partners are always in the same world, even if simultaneous scenes are going on.
>
> • Relationships may be either direct or indirect or both.
>
> • Partners relate in time, space, shape, and dynamics, all the time, and these are either contrasted or similar.
>
> • Listen. Always know what your partners are doing. Pay attention to detail.
>
> • Every action is a stone that is being laid down and may be retrieved and explored again.

• At some point, I'll give you a two-minute cue to end.

The **Superscore** list seems like a list of things to do. It's not. It's the way we remind ourselves of what's always going on.

Notes:

*Let awareness direct you. Let it shift or transform. Your aware-
ness will decide to stay with something for a long time, or talk,
or make a sound. Awareness responds to you and your partner.
Relax. Let awareness improvise.*

*If a voice or character feels false, experience that falseness, go
with the sensations of what you call "falseness." Then the experience will no longer be false.*

*Techniques are tools for efficiency. The performer must tran-
scend techniques in order to engage in the moment-to-moment
sensations of experience.*

Feelings aren't in any hurry. It's the ideas that rush along.

*A person quietly resides inside changing phenomena. Occa-
sionally, she notices the phenomena. Occasionally, she thinks she
is the phenomena itself. But, sometimes she experiences herself
pretending to be a person pretending to identify with the phenomena. From this curious detachment, she performs.*

The final score of the twenty day training, **Dreams**, often invites personal material. The students have become a community. They've
travelled through intimate and exposing experiences together. They've
been seen and they've seen into each other. They've been privy to watching themselves with great perspective. They are less attached to their
judgments, their personalities, and even to the events and circumstances
which make up their lives. They've been willing to play with it all week
after week. Now, they play very skillfully.

20C. Performance Score: Dreams

• Everyone leave the floor. We're going to make dreams. You will each get
a turn being a central figure in a dream.

• Here's how we proceed:

• One of you will go onto the floor and begin a dream by doing something that feels right to you, at the moment. Anything. You're the dreamer, the primary focus, for this improvisation, even though it will become a collaboration between yourself and anyone who enters your dream.

• You'll have a few moments by yourself. Then, anyone in the audience can enter or exit your dream at any time. Everyone on the floor is collaborating on the flow of events. The dreamer is *not* the only one controlling, or responsible for, the events that happen. But, the dreamer is the only one who stays on the floor until the end.

• This is a Superscore with a designated central figure. So, you can remind yourself of our Superscore list.

• Since there's many of you participating in this event, we'll add a few more elements to our Superscore list of reminders:

> • Have no more than three, at the most four, different things going on at any time.
>
> • LISTEN so that everything works together.
>
> • Join or bulk up each other's actions.

• As in our sleeping dreams, allow time and space to stretch and bend, and the images to be non-linear, oddly related and sequential, or overlapping. Content (scenes) can shift suddenly. Several time and place zones can exist simultaneously.

• Make your entrances and exits clear and direct.

• At any time, the person playing dreamer can end the dream by saying, "Stop."

• When you're not on the floor, you're an active audience member, ready to jump in. So, stay involved.

Entrances and Exits

The following are examples of clear entrances and exits:

- Enter or exit while doing a task.
- Enter directly to a particular location as if you belong there and exit as if it's time to go.
- Enter or exit in a hurry, or take your time, a lot of time.
- Whatever your choice, relate it to what's going on.

The entrance and exit tactic, built into this score, hones skills of observation. Students being the audience have an external vantage point from which to view the scene. Their function is to serve the scene rather than serve themselves. With this in mind, they determine whether their input is appropriate, depending on what they perceive from their audience position. They may choose to hold off or go forward, aggressively interrupt, or secretively slide into the current images and actions.

Exits demand an overview also, but from the inside of the improvisation. What effect does their departure have on the scene? Does it weaken or strengthen it? For some, who have a tendency to overstay their effectiveness, this is a good practice. Get the job done and leave.

Humor

Ann is improvising with Hugh and Stan. They each are carrying a chair. There's a loft in the studio. Holding onto their chairs, they're following each other in a line around the room. Stan's leading. When he passes the loft, he tosses his chair up onto it. Hugh follows and tosses his chair up onto the loft. Ann wants to do the same but doesn't have the strength. She gets confused, wavers, and finally throws her chair out of the room through a nearby door.

After the improvisation, we isolate this event to discuss humor. As it happened, it was not funny, yet it could have been. We felt Ann's awk-

wardness and self-consciousness. She got stuck, confused, lost awareness inside of her predicament.

For humor to occur, the performer must disengage from her predicaments. She must see all predicaments as the circumstances of the entity,
not one's self, she's playing at the moment. Ann got lost because she identified herself too closely with the situation. She experienced her inability to toss the chair as a personal failure. She forgot she was "playing" an
entity who was unable to toss the chair. If this had been her view, the
situation could either be funny or tragic. That choice is up to her. If she
experiences it as funny and expresses a detailed confession of herself
perceiving herself inside of the predicament, then we too will experience humor with her.

Humor rides on timing. The performer feels each beat. No thoughts
or distractions blur his vision. He is in the dance of expression, moment
by moment. He expresses present awareness and if his awareness is
humorous, he will be humorous. In Action Theater, we don't run after
humor. Humor finds us.

The dreamer may say, "Stop" for one of two reasons: 1) he senses a
conclusion or, 2) he feels uncomfortable. Sometimes these dreams
become more like nightmares. If the dreamer is identifying with the
material, he may reach overload and decide to call it quits. On the other
hand, having the power to end the improvisation, in itself, elicits a certain degree of objectivity and freedom.

"Dream" is a useful word. We all do it. We all know what it means. We
all know that dreams don't necessarily reflect our everyday world. They
swirl up from a mix of embedded psychic material, beyond our control.
Using the word "dream" puts people in a place of mystery. They're more
willing to float into the nether world of the imagination, and build scenes
that bend and mix social, spatial, chronological, and linguistic organization. The personality of the performer disappears, leaving a transparent
and transforming energy that fills space with feeling and complete actions.

Dreams are chosen to be the final score of the training. Each member of the group becomes a central figure of a dream. The group has shared rich and provocative moments together. They've served each other during this process of collective and individual transformation. In offering themselves up as dreamers and by adding to each other's dream, they act from gratitude.

Afterword

I began taking notes after an experience in Ann Arbor in the 70s. I was performing a solo improvisation in a loft space. I had asked a group of people to set the stage for me. They arranged an environment full of props. One of the objects was a fairly large Raggedy Anne doll. In the course of the improvisation, I named the doll Alice. Within ten minutes, she had died and the rest of the piece was about the aftermath of her death. As I was taking a bow, I noticed three women crying and holding onto each other in the front row. Later, they came backstage and were still visibly upset. One year previous to that very night, they told me, a friend of theirs named Alice had died. Before coming to the show, they had held a memorial dinner in her honor. I was shaken. I realized that the workings of improvisation had ramifications beyond my understanding. I had to observe it very closely.

This book reflects where I am, now, in that process. It's been a long time since that evening in Ann Arbor, and I've acquired a lot of notes and questions. Every time I had thought I understood the work, a new set of questions would arise. Then, those new ones would have to be followed up. About five years ago I decided to compile some of these answers into a book, no matter what. I should have known that the book itself would offer innumerable questions. At some point, as any improvisation will, the book ended itself. It was time to stop, to collect, to polish. No more questions could be brought in.

My investigations continue. In the past three years, I've taught two five-month trainings and intend to do more. Working daily, with a group of people so intensely and extensively, takes me (and them) further into the detailed discipline of clear expression.

At some point, there might be another book that begins where this one leaves off. Until then, we improvise.

If you would like a video demonstration of some of the exercises in this book, or if you'd like to get my comments on a video of you or your group doing this work, please write to: Zap Performance Projects, 1174 Cragmont Ave., Berkeley, CA. 94708